A DASTA

The Story of One Soldier's Experience in WWII

You Are Still Beautiful, America

By Ambrose Brodus, Jr.

MONTEZUMA
PUBLISHING

San Diego, California

Published by

Montezuma Publishing
Aztec Shops Ltd.
San Diego State University
San Diego, California 92182-1701

619-594-7552

www.montezumapublishing.com

ISBN: 978-0-7442-3494-7

Publishing Manager: Kim Mazyck
Design and Layout: Lia Dearborn
Formatting: Lia Dearborn
Editing: Sandra Parsons
Cover Design: Lia Dearborn
Quality Control: Joshua Segui

ABOUT THE AUTHOR

Ambrose Brodus, Jr. served his country well during World War II, having spent approximately three years in the Army (20 months of which were spent in Europe).

He was one of 5,000 Black Soldiers serving in segregated units in Europe who stepped forward to face a fanatical German Army at the time of the Battle of the Bulge. The number of volunteers was overwhelming. Ambrose was one of the 2,221 selected by General Eisenhower's Command and became a member of a first-ever integrated U.S. Infantry. He participated in four major battles: Central Europe, Southern France, Northern France, and the Rhineland. He received the Combat Infantry Badge, the Bronze Star, the EAME Ribbon, Good Conduct Medal, and a Sharp Shooter Medal. Like many GIs, Ambrose returned to school at the end of hostilities in Europe and the Pacific.

After college he spent 13 years working in industry and later became effectively involved with the Civil Rights movement. On one occasion Ambrose was sentenced by a

court to 90 days in jail for blocking the entrance to a San Diego Bank of America in an effort to call attention to the deplorable employment practices exercised by bank officials at that time. As an active member and elected official of the Congress of Racial Equality (CORE), he helped to bring meaningful change to San Diego in the area of civil rights.

Later Ambrose responded to a request by Urban League officials to work for the San Diego Urban League, where he demonstrated talent for promoting improvement in educational opportunities for Black students and measures related to the welfare of Black people in general.

Ambrose has many awards (certificates, citations, and trophies) to grace his walls and desk. He is especially proud of the Human Dignity Award presented to him in January 2013 by the Jackie Robinson YMCA of San Diego County. This award reflects the many contributions Ambrose has made to California and the nation.

DEDICATION

This book is dedicated to my parents, Ambrose Brodus, Sr. and Pinkie Wortham Brodus; to my four sisters, Eva, Evola, Versell, and Tommie; and my brothers, Jessie and Herman. I also dedicate this book to my extended family of aunts, uncles, nieces, nephews, and cousins. Lastly, I dedicate this book to the memory of my grandparents and the generations before them who struggled and fought through the dark days of slavery, understanding full well that a better day was coming. May God bless their souls.

A Dastardly Act

TABLE OF CONTENTS

ABOUT THE AUTHOR..iii

DEDICATION..v

ACKNOWLEDGMENTS ix

SPECIAL DEDICATION xiii

INTRODUCTION 1

1   BACKGROUND, INDUCTION AND EARLY
    EXPERIENCES IN THE U.S. ARMY 5

2   A SEPARATE VOYAGE TO WAR...................17

3   NEAR THE HEAT OF BATTLE,
    UNRECOGNIZED AND DISRESPECTED 27

    The 377th Crosses the Channel 31

4   THE GENERAL'S INVITATION AND THE
    BLACK SOLDIERS' RESPONSES 43

    Inspirational Recall...................................65

5   WAR'S END AND RECONCILIATION 81

6   A BITTERSWEET RETURN TO HOME.........105

7   AN HONORABLE DISCHARGE IN A
    DISHONORABLE MANNER........................135

8   ON WITH LIFE AND HOPE FOR
    A BETTER FUTURE....................................145

9   AT LAST: RECOGNITION AND
    APPRECIATION 155

10 REFLECTIONS OF GRADUAL
    PROGRESS 167

      Black Officer Firsts 169

      More History...169

SELECTED REFERENCES FOR A
BROADER VIEW OF AMERICAN MILITARY
HISTORY OF BLACK TROOPS IN WAR AND
RELATED DATA 179

ACKNOWLEDGMENTS

From the beginning of this project, Rosa Maxwell was right there by my side, as focused as anyone could be in getting the first draft manuscript prepared for review. She did it in a manner consistent with professional expertise and friendship. She never complained about the lengthy yellow pages, as I do the old fashioned, long-hand writing to arouse my memory and convey my thoughts. Rosa managed to handle it, no matter how the material was presented to her. I am deeply appreciative of that.

Rosa Maxwell passed away prior to completion of the final draft of the manuscript for this book. I immediately put the work aside for several months. Eventually I regained strength and resumed work and to my delight, a high-spirited young person came onto the scene, and I am very pleased with her performance. Congratulations Noni Yeldell.

My wife Lois often sits long hours at the breakfast table during early mornings and mid-afternoons while I am at a desk down the hall, struggling with my thoughts, trying to bring up facts from years" past. The fact that I am able to have a clear view of many things that passed my way

when I was really young must be attributed to the quiet Lois allows me to have when I am on concentration cruise control. She doesn't interfere much. I am happy with that and I appreciate her understanding.

Although the basic materials and ideas for this work have come from the inner recesses of my mind, from memories long since stored away for safekeeping, I managed to find ample support and corroborating data at two local libraries—the Malcolm X Library in San Diego, CA and the San Diego County Library in Bonita, CA. The staff at each facility was very helpful to me, even though I never mentioned this project to them. Thanks for their support. At these libraries I secured documents that gave me the names of key German officers responsible for certain military assaults on Allied Units during the war, and other significant data that affected me there.

Prior to 2007 there was very little discussion in my circles regarding my experiences in the army. But once the word was out that I had something to say, a few close friends politely raised their voices, encouraging me to write this book. So, without calling any names, here's my thanks to them. I appreciate their strong support.

Acknowledgments

Dr. Dorothy L.W. Smith graciously consented to read the manuscript and offer structural suggestions. Her review helped immensely. I thank you, Dr. Smith, for your contributions to this work.

A Dastardly Act

SPECIAL DEDICATION

This is a special attempt to convey a message to those men who volunteered to face the fanatical German Army at a critical time during this war, as well as their families, and comes with humility and pride. I am happy to be a part of your extended family. This book is also dedicated to you. The 2,221 Negro Volunteers who were chosen by General Dwight D. Eisenhower's staff were assigned to the following Divisions, 1st, 2nd, 8th, 9th, 12th, 14th, 19th, 69th, 78th, 99th, and 104th, where they joined ranks with all-White troops and immediately proceeded to honor the General's "desire" to destroy the enemy forces and end hostilities without delay.

A Dastardly Act

Below is a partial list of my associates and friends from the 19th Armored Infantry Battalion, Company 4. These are the ones whose names I can remember as I have seen only three of them since our discharge from the army.

Archer, Ross L.	Morehand, Charles M.
Boger, Charles W.	McComb, John S.
Curl, William Jr.	Nelson, Elijah
Daniels, Douglas F.	Richardson, Williams H.
Davis, Ecleza F.	Scott, Theodoro R.
Dodson, Willie H.	Smith, Raymond H.
Durroh, James	Shields, Oliver V.
Facon, George	Taryer, Clifton
Frierson, Willie C.	Tate, Percy
Gordon, Chafe T.	Walters, John
Henderson, Damon Jr.	Watkins, Raymond
Henderson, Elbert	Williams, George R.
Hutchinson, Minuard	Williams, John S.
Jackson, Robert L.	Wilson, Willie M.

INTRODUCTION

Documenting my experiences in the Army of the United States of America was assembled for two primary reasons: (1) to provide my family with basic information about my life for the period of time I served my country, at home and in foreign countries, and do it with a degree of clarity that I and they would be comfortable with; and (2) to aid the Association of the 2,221 Negro Infantry Volunteers of WWII in their effort to make known to the world an episode in U.S. military history that is known to only a very few—an episode that, due to its historical nature, ought to be told.

When I returned home from the war in Europe in mid-August 1945, I didn't talk about what I saw or did in that foreign land. My parents didn't ask a lot of questions and, when we did talk about Europe, I usually focused on the more pleasant things. Rarely did I discuss anything about the horrors I encountered, the issues of segregation, or the general discomforts of war. I never came close to repeating the often expressed axiom that, "war is hell."

On one occasion several weeks following my discharge from the army, my Mother handed me a letter

I had written her and Dad from France or Germany. The letter had implications of combat activity without specificity. I had forgotten about that letter, but the moment I began to read it I remembered what I had made reference to. My mother gently asked if I would explain it. I tried. During the course of my explanation, I recall emphasizing that we were fighting a war. She listened quietly. I think she knew I was not telling all! She seemed to accept that with the understanding and care that mothers possess.

Dad didn't ask the questions. His son was home safe, thank God! I brought home from Germany a 32-Caliber automatic pistol I was glad to be able to give him as a gift. I would like to have talked more and done more for both of my parents at that time.

But in August 1945, I was just a 20-year-old kid, returning from a war zone where I and every other Negro service member in uniform had confronted the all-American dilemma—racial segregation and discrimination—while serving our country. In Europe, some of us had taken advantage of an opportunity to integrate a segment of the U.S. Military in a combat configuration. Post-war reviews showed that we performed well and that our efforts contributed significantly to the successful conclusion

of the war with Adolph Hitler in favor of the Allies. But when the war in Europe ended, events that happened to those previously segregated U.S. soldiers who courageously stepped forward when given the opportunity at the time of the Fuhrer's massive counter offensive in Belgium, December 1944 was another shameful chapter in American military history. The plight of those 2,221 African American combat veterans became a non-issue as far as the U.S. government was concerned. That is, until Bill Clinton was elected president. This memoir is one part of my effort to help spread the word about a part of American military history that the world should know about.

A Dastardly Act

CHAPTER 1

BACKGROUND, INDUCTION AND EARLY EXPERIENCES IN THE U.S. ARMY

I am Ambrose Brodus, Jr., the first son of Ambrose Brodus, Sr., and Pinkie Wortham Brodus, born January 6, 1925 in Minden, Louisiana, in Webster Parrish. I am told that my birth enlightened the hearts of the Brodus and Wortham family members far and near, as they acknowledged the fulfillment of a legacy. Like all African American youth growing up and pursuing an education in Louisiana in the days of racial segregation, I attended and graduated from the prestigious, but segregated, Webster High School. It was the only high school for "Colored" in Webster Parish. While I was never content with segregation and its negative effects, I, like all Negro youth growing up in that dual social system, learned early on the true nature of the system and determined that it would not last forever. How long? I don't recall anyone setting a time for its demise. Our parents taught us that

we were as good as anybody else, to respect adults, obey the law, and be a good neighbor. We learned early in life to observe all things, especially when in contact with White people.

We attended our segregated schools to learn and become proficient in curriculum matters presented to us. We made an effort to hear it all. Some things attracted my attention more than others, which is normal for most youth. However, while engaged in a discussion of world affairs in a social studies class in 1942, the teacher emphasized the activities and behaviors of the German leader, Adolf Hitler, which seemed cruel and unusual to me. I remember thinking, "This is a very bad man," and made a special mental note of the things I learned that day.

After turning eighteen years of age, I was inducted into the U.S. Army on June 17, 1943. The date of my actual entry to active service was June 24, 1943, at Shreveport, Louisiana. From Shreveport, along with a group of approximately 40 other Negro youth, I was transported to Camp Beauregard, near Alexandria, Louisiana, where we spent several days in preparation for assignment to other military facilities to begin basic training. While at Beauregard, there were a number of minor race-related incidents that gave me some idea of the things we might experience as we proceeded in the service.

Although Negro and White inductees were separated (segregated) in all phases of the processing, especially during duty hours, the two groups did manage to come together to some extent on occasion. Two instances bear mention here. One evening as both groups gathered on the athletic field for a sports activity, there was friendly conversation about sports and things in general. Later, someone found two pairs of boxing gloves and in no time we had a friendly boxing contest. A large circle was drawn on the ground to represent the ring. Inside the ring was one White and one Black youth. We all gathered around the circle, Whites on one side, Blacks on the other. One White agreed to referee the match. As the contest began, someone with a watch kept the time. Round One was good and clean. Round Two was exciting. Round Three seemed to be a bit tiring for the White youth and, as that round ended, several White youths pulled their buddy off to the side and dipped his gloves into the sand. Apparently they thought we didn't see that. We did, however, and also dipped our guy's gloves in the sand. We were ready for Round Four and more. When the Whites noticed the sand on our guy's gloves, they hollered foul

play. Round Four didn't begin when an officer came to the scene and put a stop to what was beginning to be our first integration experience in the U.S. Army.

The other incident of note occurred in a general purpose building where servicemen with performing arts talent assembled during free time to practice. One evening a group of Negro and White youth with an interest in music assembled with a variety of musical instruments and started a little jam session. There were drums, saxophones, trombones, etc. I had a trumpet. Just as we were beginning to sound a little interesting, an officer arrived and broke it up. It was a friendly activity, but the officer explained that the laws of the State of Louisiana prohibited social mixing among the races. That ended that experiment. Another opportunity lost.

How interesting these two episodes were—so much the same and yet potentially, significantly different. However, when viewed from the perspective of a seasoned observer, one might say that this simply was the nature and function of the dual social system. That being the case, the system has had a difficult time determining its direction and has failed to acknowledge the limits of the function.

The next day I was assigned to a group traveling north to a camp where we would begin basic training and traveled by train to Washington, D.C. Already I was enjoying some benefits of my induction into the military of my country. We made a brief stop in St. Louis, Missouri and were able to get off the train and view some of the sites. The Mississippi River held my attention longer than anything else in the area. It was like reviewing geography class all over, except this was a field trip. How wonderful that was. Only the hot scrambled egg and sausage sandwich I had for lunch as we prepared to leave the area linger as long in my memory of that stop in St. Louis as the view of the Mississippi river.

Our arrival in Washington was another great and pleasant surprise. Here we were in the nation's capital, the place where so much history had been made—the place where the very fate of my people was debated and critical discussions regarding world affairs confirmed. This was quite a bit for an 18-year old Negro kid out of Louisiana for the first time to take in. The kid took a deep breath and moved forward, remembering all the time the teachings of his parents and the advice of those young teachers in those segregated schools that Louisiana laws restricted him to. I felt comfortable and had no reservations about being

exposed to this new environment. It was all very educational and I considered myself to be a quick learner.

From the train station at D.C. we were taken by bus to Fort Belvoir, Virginia, where we would begin 90 days of intense basic training. As we lined up under orders from a sergeant to begin our march from the train to buses a distance away, I noticed a half-dozen White youth ages 8-10 walking along beside us, simulating orders. They counted cadence for half the distance to the buses. They were White and we were Black. I wondered about that for a moment and then kicked it aside but I'll admit that their presence and their act came close to bugging me. I was pleased they weren't allowed to continue on.

Ft. Belvoir was a facility well known for producing engineers. This was basic training and company commanders didn't waste time getting to the basics: there was a lot to learn and I made an effort to get it all right, but getting adjusted to barracks life did require some effort. Training to become physically fit was serious work, but a lot of fun; that is, until they introduced the long-distance hikes. The 5-mile hike I could handle pretty well, but then came the longer ones, including the 40-mile events. Learning to handle the rifle, breaking it down and reassembling it was something I enjoyed doing, and firing on the rifle range was an experience almost everyone looked forward to. I got to be pretty good at that. I didn't make expert though. The basic infantry training was exciting. I learned a lot that was helpful to me months later in Europe.

On completion of training, where I earned the Sharpshooter Badge on the rifle range and was assigned the Military Occupational Specialties, Bugler 803 and Carpenter 050 designations, I was given a 15-day leave to go home for a visit with my family. I enjoyed that little break very much. Besides visiting with family, I managed to spend a little time with the young girl who, years later, became my wife. When I returned from leave I reported to a site in nearby Maryland where I was assigned to the 377th Engineering Battalion. A few days later, the 377th was moved to Camp Shanks, New York, where we were to be processed for duty overseas.

The two weeks I spent at Camp Shanks allowed me time to visit other close family members who lived in the New York area. These included two sisters, three aunts, a grandfather whom I had never met, an uncle, and many cousins. This little brother, in New York in a military uniform, was treated royally. It seemed that they took me everywhere: the Statue of Liberty, Times Square,

Rockefeller Center, the Rockets, Harlem, the League of Nations headquarters that became the United Nations headquarters after the end of the war, the Apollo Theater, Coney Island, and many other places. I quickly began to feel like somebody special. Meeting those relatives I had never seen before was a delightful experience. These included a sister of my father who left Louisiana about the time of my birth; my father's youngest sister who was born in New York, and my grandfather (Dad's father), who relocated to New York when my father was a very young man and raised another family. I learned not long ago the reason for my grandfather's leaving the state of Louisiana and not returning. It seems that he had a difference of opinion on some local issues. Two men set out to harm him. He won and they lost.

While waiting for orders, I learned that my grandfather was ill and hospitalized in New Jersey. Members of the family planned to visit him on the coming Sunday. The plan was to meet at Penn Station, 33rd & 7th Avenue, and take the train from there to New Jersey to see grandfather. I was encouraged to join the group for this visit. I was delighted with the thought of meeting my grandfather and possibly others I had never met. I placed a call to my sisters in Brooklyn to let them know I could get a pass to leave camp for the weekend. As usual they gave me an update on travel plans, what to expect, etc. On Sunday, like a smooth running clock, family members gathered at the train station in Manhattan at the designated time. They came from the Bronx, Long Island, Brooklyn, and Harlem. There were about eight or ten in the group and me, in my uniform. I was introduced to those I had not met before. I was happy, quiet, and observing. I paid attention to everything. My sisters, Eva and Evola, took turns explaining the various sites and activities to me along the route to New Jersey. I remembered the weather being sunny and pleasant. Everything was super. Yet, thoughts of my purpose for being in New York in the first place kept creeping across the forefront of my mind. And while I wouldn't make a conscious effort to push those thoughts aside, I was affected a little. However, there was never a time when I was confused about this, as I said to myself on numerous occasions, "I know why I am here," and I was pleased with that. I never forgot the big picture. I would be headed overseas soon and I was prepared for that.

We had arrived at our destination, everyone accounted for. We headed toward the hospital administration center. As we walked into the building I could feel the warmth of

family—full of compassion and determined. Approaching grandfather's room, the quiet conversation became quieter. Those who spoke were the seniors of the group, like Aunt Clifford. She was about 40 at the time and in excellent command of the English language. She had a clear, powerful voice and when she spoke, people listened. Aunt Clifford led us into the room.

The daughters greeted their father first. The grandchildren followed. Since I was the stranger in the group, I had to be introduced. I waited my turn patiently. My oldest sister Eva Brodus Williams had the pleasure of making the introduction. When she called me forward I was shaking a bit, but that disappeared the second I saw his face. Eva said, "Granddad, this is your grandson, Ambrose Brodus, Jr." He spoke softly with a "Hello, how are you?" I really don't recall how I responded or what specifically I said, but I presume it was something appropriate. I am confident it was. There might have been a tear in his eye. I felt good about this introduction—Ambrose Brodus, Jr., meeting for the first time ever, George Washington Brodus, the father of his father—a scene to be remembered and something I will never forget. Immediately I could see my father's features in his face. I hope he was impressed with me in my military uniform and in the fact that his grandson would soon be heading off to represent his country in a foreign land.

That was a fact that all family members were aware of and their warm response and compassion provided a reservoir of strength for me for that time and the future. At the end of the day in New Jersey, we parted with best wishes and I returned to my barracks at Camp Shanks.

I felt so very comfortable in the knowledge that I was closely surrounded by so many wonderful and loving relatives. I had been blessed to have two weekend trips into the city and, with the Thanksgiving holiday coming up in a few days, my sisters had invited me to return for Thanksgiving dinner. I looked forward to that. However, my streak of good fortune vanished the day following my return from the family visit with Grandfather. My unit received orders to go. No phone calls out, no calls in. This was it. I accepted that news like a soldier should. Duty called. I wondered though how my sisters would feel when I didn't show up for Thanksgiving Day. After a moment or two I determined they would figure it out and proceed with their dinner. I knew they would say a prayer for me.

On November 23, 1943, sometime around midnight my unit, the 377th Engineering Battalion, boarded the Luxury Liner the *Queen Elizabeth*. The *Queen* had been converted to a troop ship, equipped to carry 25,000 service members. It was far from being a luxury now with 25,000 young men aboard, each carrying a huge pack on his back.

CHAPTER 2

A SEPARATE VOYAGE TO WAR

As a youth coming out of Louisiana and a strictly segregated South, I observed everything around me and made a mental note of the more significant things, especially those things related to race. My unit, every man in full gear, marched through the streets at midnight toward the port where we would board the *Queen Elizabeth*. Some units stood in formation along sidewalks while others kept pace in parking lots, waiting their turn to board. Just as we passed one White unit, a single voice hollered out, "Where y'all boys going?" Quickly, and resolutely, a deep voice rang out from someone in our midst, "To see your Mama." No response to that. The only sound from that moment was the sound of boots on the pavement, moving toward the ship. That was awesome! This Black guy responding to a White guy in a public place in a manner like that was, to me, really something. While I had never used that language myself, I

recognized it right away and understood its meaning. The boys in the streets called it the "dozen" or "dozens," as if one dozen is not enough! It's talking bad about someone's parents, especially one's mother. It is meant to hurt. It's a way of getting back at somebody who has offended you, or a way to start a fight with someone you don't respect.

As the question was uttered, I wondered why he did that. Thinking rationally, some might say the guy didn't mean any harm; it was his way of injecting a little humor into the situation. Whatever his motive, he chose the wrong place, the wrong time, and the wrong group to ask. He probably learned something from that. A day later I learned the identity of the person who responded to that racist question, Douglas Daniels. Douglas and I became good friends and members of the same company and platoon with the 377th.

In a period of a few hours the 377th was all aboard the mighty *Queen Elizabeth*. Truly amazing. Unthinkable two years earlier, but there I was, and there we were, heading out to sea before dawn. It didn't matter much that accommodations were cramped. We were the United States Army and we were off to war to protect our country. That thought invigorated me.

At breakfast call on the first day at sea we were awakened by a platoon sergeant. I got up and joined the long line to get a meal that was not the most desirable. The dining room was packed. At that time I hadn't learned the names of many in my new platoon, so I had very little conversation; I just observed everything and followed orders. By this time, even on the first day, sickness had begun to set in. Some guys had difficulty holding their food. Medics passed out salt tablets, but that was not helpful for some. We all had to adjust to the new experience. I made it back to the cramped quarters where the only thing one could do was sit on his bunker and read a book if he could find one. I found a magazine.

Hours passed before we were given the opportunity to go up on deck where we could breathe fresh air. What a treat that was. We felt much better now that we could see the vast ocean and breathe fresh air. We could think about a lot of things, like family, training, destination, etc. Surely my thoughts were about family, initially my parents and younger brother and sister I left there in Minden. I was hoping they were not worrying too much about me. I knew they were praying for me, that was a given. Then I began to think about my sisters there in New York and the others.

Eva and Evola were expecting me in Brooklyn on Thursday
to have Thanksgiving dinner with them. I imagined the
various delicacies that would be on their dinner table. I
didn't feel badly for myself. I knew there would be another
day. The focus now was on the present. We were in the
middle of this vast ocean and no one had told us where we
were going and what we should expect when we got there.
However, knowing that we were in the Atlantic Ocean,
aboard the *Queen Elizabeth* was a pretty good clue as to
where we might be headed.

While on deck I made one glaring observation—only
Negro soldiers were present. No White service members in
sight. Viewing this scene one could imagine we owned this
baby. In a sense we owned the deck while we were there.
A thought okay for contemporary consideration perhaps,
but my thoughts were much deeper than that—there were
25,000 troops on board this great and respected vessel
with two separate (segregated) armies, representing one
country, headed to war to fight a common enemy in one
war. I wondered if anyone was thinking about the potential
problems. Honestly I never saw any appreciable signs of
interest or concern regarding racial issues except the act of
keeping Blacks and Whites apart.

On arrival at our apparent destination before dawn
on the seventh day of the voyage we learned quickly that
we were, in fact, at a port on the western coast of England.
I believe it was in the Liverpool area. We had crossed the
Atlantic Ocean at a time when enemy submarines were out
there in large numbers searching for allied ships in order
to destroy them. We did this without benefit of the usual
naval escort that smaller ships required because the speed
of the *Queen Elizabeth* enabled her to outrun any of those
submerged vessels. "Power to the Queen," I thought with
great appreciation. I was aware that before our departure a
New York newspaper reported on the high level of German
submarines in the Atlantic. I don't think I was ready for that
kind of encounter yet.

Before daybreak we were off the ship and loaded onto
trains of the British Railway, headed south to a makeshift
camp. It was late November and the weather was cloudy,
damp, and cold. We couldn't concern ourselves much about
that: we had work to do. That was a task and I accepted it.
Later we moved into the regional area of Southampton where
we were more prominently housed at a small camp within
a few miles of the English Channel. We remained there
for several weeks engaged in a variety of duties, including

training. During this time we had an opportunity to meet and become somewhat acquainted with some British citizens, most of whom had jobs on site or at nearby businesses. The British equivalent of the USO (United Service Organization) occasionally provided tea and tarts for our unit at a local hall. Sometimes a movie was shown. While this service was not something one would care to shout about, it was helpful for our morale. There was no such thing as liberty to visit a local town or city at this time, which further limited or delayed opportunities for open discussion with the citizenry.

This situation changed somewhat as spring came and we moved a bit further southwest toward the Channel. As one might notice, we moved around a lot. In one area we spent enough time to build a small camp for more incoming soldiers. We built this facility in an area near a castle that some said was the possession of the English philosopher and mathematician Sir Isaac Newton (1643-1727). The castle was an interesting piece of property, but I don't recall that any of us ever ventured inside. Had we done so, it might have served as base for very interesting conversation. It was a nostalgic experience just being in the area. As I recall, it was in this area that I drank my first beer.

There was a small village nearby, about two miles from camp, and some evenings after duty a group of us would walk to the village to learn more about our neighbors. We stopped at the first pub (beer tavern) we saw and the people inside welcomed us enthusiastically. They were mostly old men and women. The younger British were away in service for their country. Live accordion music was very popular in these pubs. People drank beer, played darts, and ate fish and chips. They had fun and invited our group to join in. We did. We talked about America and a little about the war. I don't recall any discussion about race during these initial contacts with this group. Discussions were primarily social and lighthearted. No politics.

When the new buildings were completed at this site we packed up and moved to another location a few miles away. Newly arriving U.S. soldiers began occupying the camp as soon as we moved out. Several days after we moved to a location near Bristol, three of us were given an assignment that took us back near the recently completed camp. We decided to walk through the area to use the restroom. Before we could finish, a White officer came up in a rage and attempted to admonish us for using the toilet. "White and Negro soldiers don't use the same facilities."

After explaining to him that "We built this place," he was still furious. His words didn't mean much to us. We left what we had deposited for him to clean up. The unit he commanded was all White. No further response from him. *Mental note number 47.*

Between March and late April the 377th moved around much more, as did most U.S. Army units in Great Britain. All were training and preparing for the invasion of France. These activities took us through and around the cities of Plymouth, Bristol, Exeter, and many smaller towns and villages. We never shared a training site or military base with a White group, though we would occasionally pass a White group on the highway. Even during the few times our group would get rest and recuperation (R&R) for a few hours in a town, we would mostly have the streets to ourselves. There was a plan to keep White and Negro troops separated, which was carefully observed.

When we were in town most businesses remained open as usual. However, I did see some restaurants close their doors and put up "Closed for Business" signs on doors and windows when we showed up. We said then that those were the ones that had been brainwashed; White America had taught them pretty well. What a position they took. We were there in their country to help protect them. We handled it all. We knew our overall purpose. It was, however, these kinds of situations that contributed to the frustrations and open clashes between Negro and White troops in cities all over England.

In spite of our efforts to remain calm in the midst of a difficult situation, it exploded for us late one evening when my Negro company was taken to a seaport town to see a movie. After arriving in town, we were required to wait a half-block away from the theater while the White soldiers completed their turn viewing the movie. By now it was dusk and we were getting weary. When the movie ended the White soldiers had to walk past us to reach their vehicles. Words were exchanged and a small war ensued. In ten minutes it was over. Blood was spilled, energy wasted, and feelings were hurt. Nobody in our group sustained an injury. We anticipated events like this, but no planning was involved, just remember a scout's motto: be prepared.

What happened there was a reflection of incidents occurring in communities throughout England during those times, including London. While these affairs were not helpful to the allied war effort, they surely did help us to maintain our self-respect. Given the nature of our

circumstances there, maintaining self-respect was critical. Our commanding officer in the region didn't seem to have a clue as to how the issue might be seriously addressed. At least from my perspective I saw nothing to that effect. I suspect the Nazis, who were all around us, were paying close attention. *Mental note number 60, documented.*

At all times, I tried to keep my mind focused on our purpose for being in that beautiful country, even though it involved imagining the absence of so much military and so much secrecy. I always felt comfortable with the level of focus I was able to maintain. I think that was true for my comrades as well.

CHAPTER 3

NEAR THE HEAT OF BATTLE,
UNRECOGNIZED AND DISRESPECTED

By early May we began to feel that our purpose for "being there" in Europe was coming closer to realization. Our leader, Supreme Allied Commander General Dwight D. Eisenhower and the British Command had been planning for the invasion of France to take back the country that Adolf Hitler had possessed since his troops enforced their rule on the French in June, 1940. The United States' presence in Britain and its strong support of the powerful British military machine had helped keep the Germans' Fuhrer at bay until the appropriate campaign could be organized. Everyone in the world knew that Allied Forces in Europe were preparing for a serious attack on the French coast, across the English Channel. Every military person in the area, whether on land or at sea, felt that he had a role in what was about to come down. Some knew the specifics of

their role, some knew little, and still others knew nothing except having obligations to be prepared to do something when called on. What no one knew except the elite few, and I am assuming that those would be among General Eisenhower's inner circle, was the date, place, and time the invasion would begin. No one, including people at the U.S. Army publication *Stars and Stripes* knew, and if they knew, they were not talking. At least there is no evidence that they were talking.

German bombs kept falling on coastal cities of Britain and Allied air power continued pounding German targets. We could feel the tempo of the war picking up day after day, but we, the everyday soldier, had little information about the overall scheme of things, only knowing about those things going on around us. For instance, in early May we pitched camp in an area about 45 minutes walking distance to the Channel. We walked that distance in light gear for the first few days, returning to camp at night. That pattern continued into early June.

On June 5 we marched to the coast and didn't march back to camp that evening. We spent the night on the low cliffs overlooking the beach. At about 4:00 a.m. the next morning we were awakened by the distant sound of big guns from American and British ships blasting the French coast and planes dropping bombs on targets in Cherbourg and Le Havre in Normandy. The invasion was on. We raced down the cliff and across the beach to the edge of the water, but all we could see was lots of black smoke and hear the sound of machinery and the blast of guns. We watched for a while. I can't say for how long. There was little conversation among us. As for my thoughts, I don't remember the specifics, and I acknowledge that the initial banging was one hell-of-a wakeup call. Nothing will ever compare with that. I do want to remember that experience for the rest of my life. Thoughts beyond there were basic and random, like, "Are the boats coming to pick us up and, if so, how soon? Where are the orders from the company commander or platoon leader? Tell me something. We, I, have a need to know." These thoughts surfaced and continued for a while. Then I remembered, "This is the Army." I soon reconciled to that fact and later, near daybreak, I joined my platoon and we retraced our steps back up the cliff to collect our gear and wait for orders.

My thoughts were awesome. It's still dark and on the water you can't see much, but you know this is D-Day. Allied troops are landing on the beaches of France and

German soldiers are fighting like hell to prevent it. Soldiers are dying and we know we have a task to do. We will handle it when the time comes. When will they call for us? This is war. We go when we are called. Yep. Such thoughts repeat themselves, time and time again, never finding satisfaction with a response.

They didn't call our number that day. As a matter of fact, about three weeks passed before the 377th crossed the English Channel. We waited in the same little camp we had occupied for a few months prior to the invasion. We were there with anticipation not easy to describe, at times huddled around radios, anxiously trying to get word of the fighting just 28 miles across that pond. At times the news came slowly. Other times it would come in abundance. Most times what we heard was positive. There were times, however, when the news was not good, like the battle for Saint-Lo, a heavily fortified area inland a ways from the coast. The Germans pulled tricks out of the bag, it seemed. Our troops were dying and there was nothing we could do about that from where we were standing.

The months that we had been in England preparing for D-Day provided opportunity for us to learn something about the countries of Europe, the people, their culture and their languages. As for the Germans, we also learned something about their combat skills. They were good. We knew they had some fanatic units who, with their zeal and commitment to Hitler, would go to the extreme and beyond in an attempt to defeat an opponent. All of this was good information to have; still such awareness could cause concerns. Nevertheless, our attitudes remained positive because "Our cause was the better cause." In time, our troops defeated the Germans in the battle for Saint-Lo and the front lines moved forward.

The 377th Crosses the Channel

By the time we landed, the coastal towns and villages had been liberated by American and British forces. Many Allied and enemy soldiers had died on the beaches. American and British troops were moving methodically toward Reims and Paris. Bodies of the fallen had been cleared from the area. However, clear evidence of battle remained. As I put my feet on French soil that morning, my thoughts immediately shifted to the spot where I stood on the British side of the Channel on D-Day, about 4:00 a.m. I had no control of those thoughts at that moment. It was all about what I envisioned happening in the area that "I now occupied." Awesome could only be the beginning of a description.

Within a short time of our landing on the French coast, things began to happen that enabled me to have a clearer understanding and appreciation for the vast amount of planning accomplished by General Eisenhower and his Allied staff in preparation for the campaign to defeat the most despicable man in the world. From the time of my arrival in England at the age of 18, I had managed to observe many things and I had learned a lot. True, there was much more I did not know, but I made assumptions to fill in the blanks and, to some extent, that served my purpose pretty well. I had some appreciable sense of what was going on. Within a few hours of our landing in Normandy, U.S. Army trucks pulled up to a nearby area to take us to a train station several miles away where we board a train to ride farther inland. The front lines had moved beyond Saint-Lo.

Following an amazing train ride we arrived somewhere in the vicinity of Reims. From there the 377th took its place in the grand scheme of the military operation in France. As a non-combat engineering unit, we moved about performing a variety of essential military services behind the front lines. Much of the enemy had been killed or taken prisoner in most of these areas, but there were still hot spots that required some form of combat action. The French city of Metz near the German border was one of these. Allied troops were moving fast toward the German border city of Saarbrucken, and guns, ammunition, and other supplies had to keep pace with that movement.

The Red Ball Express, an army-trucking unit, moved an average of 12,500 pounds of supplies every day from the French docks to the front lines in record time. Almost 75% of the drivers were Black soldiers. After 83 days, the army (being as resourceful as they were), decided to make use of the French railway to aid that cause. Some of the railway had been damaged by Allied air raids on German forces while they occupied the country. Other damage might have been caused by German commanders as they withdrew from fast-advancing Allied armored divisions. Whatever the cause, repairs had to be made. The 377th, with its engineering skills, was called on to repair rail lines on a key bridge at the city of Metz. We took it on under threat of sniper fire, but the damage to the bridge and related rails was completed in record time. The Army was then able to increase the forward movement of critical supplies to the front lines, augmenting the outstanding work of the Red Ball Express. The word was out that these guys worked

24-hour shifts at times to ensure that the men up front got the stuff they needed to win the battles.

During the next six or eight weeks, we had duty in diverse areas of France, including Burgundy and Alsace Lorraine. We also spent some time in the quaint little city of Dijon, which we discovered had been the Gestapo Headquarters in France since the 1940 invasion and takeover. The German secret police moved out of Dijon just ahead of advancing Allied combat troops before our arrival on the scene. On their way out of town they left morbid evidence they had been there, committing atrocities against civilians and suspected members of the French underground. While we set up a quick camp in the area, we were reminded of the capacity of these guys: *be alert. Be prepared.* Nobody moved a step without his M-1. Even with such caution we lost one friend in Dijon. The discovery of the naked body of one of our guys came early on the morning we were packing to relocate to another site. We were aware that German officers were trying to infiltrate the U.S. Army. Some had already been caught in army uniforms, hanging out behind Allied troop lines, trying to pass as American soldiers. Conceivably they could do a variety of things that might have some negative impact on the conduct of the war or of a given battle. The night prior to our departure from Dijon someone caught one of our guys off guard, killed him, took his uniform, dumped his body, and quickly disappeared. How could that happen one might ask? It's war! A Gestapo officer in civilian clothes might have passed as a friendly Frenchman with a bottle of wine. You blink. Game over!

The constant movement of this unit as with other service units was, in my view, a good indication of success in front line action, especially when that movement is generally forward. Although lateral movement is often a strategy tactic, forward is net gain. An army private having no responsibility for making profound decisions regarding "East or West" troop movements, I still had no difficulty determining "net." After Dijon I developed a pretty good concept of how the war in Europe was going. Obviously, we were winning. There had been a lot of movement forward and all service units were participating. I began to think about some of those Signal Corps, Ordinance, Medical, Engineers, Trucking, and Quartermaster Units. They all had roles to play in this war.

I became alarmed one day in August when I was given a copy of the latest edition of the army's publication,

Stars and Stripes. To my amazement there was a column on the front over, in "bold" letters that read, "REAR ECHELON COWBOYS" roam the range. The column seemed to focus in a negative way on the task and performance of U.S. Army servicemen in service units in France. I could not believe this, a U.S. Army publication circulating in the country where war was being conducted would write negatively and derisively about its own countrymen. The article also had a racial connotation. I suspect the enemy took note of that article. I remember, it was shameful. There were many service units in France and other countries in the European Theatre of Operations during this war, all performing important and necessary tasks. Included among these was the Red Ball Express. This elite group of segregated Negro soldiers was very visible as they were responsible for moving, ammunition, and other supplies from ships to front-line troops in a manner that ensured the units up front always had what they needed to fight Hitler's army. The high caliber performance of segregated servicemen like those in the Red Ball Express and other units were vital in assuring victory for the Allies in WWII. No one can take that away, not even the *Stars and Stripes.*

Chapter 3

I was extremely disturbed when I saw the article, but there was nothing I could do about it. I tucked it away, but I never forgot about it. Many years later, after I learned that the late Andy Rooney, author and CBS reporter, had served on the staff of the *Stars and Stripes* during WWII and that he had spent time in Europe, I decided to write him a letter to see if he remembered the article. I wondered if he had anything to do with the article. I needed to know. I wrote the letter and mailed it to the CBS address in New York. At about the same time, I learned that Rooney was ill. He passed away shortly thereafter. I never received a response to my letter. I had anticipated hearing from Andy Rooney because if anyone at *Stars and Stripes* who had been with the publication remembered the article, he would be the one. I had researched Rooney's time in the army. He indeed did write for the *Stars and Stripes* during WWII while in Europe. In fact, his performance with the publication was outstanding.

According to one of his books, *The Fortunes of War*, Rooney landed on Utah Beach with the second wave several days after D-day. He covered and wrote stories about the Battle at Saint-Lo and was among the first group of reporters to enter Paris. He received a Bronze Star for his

A Dastardly Act

reporting of the Battle of Saint-Lo. Andy Rooney's service as a military reporter put him in close association with people like Earnest Hemingway, Ernie Pyle, and Charles Collingwood who, as civilians, reported news of the war to the major wire services and other publications. Rooney was a military reporter and apparently an aggressive one at that. The research strongly suggests that he could have been involved in the writing of the article in reference here. I saw an article in another one of Rooney's book, *My War*, and found the phrase "Rear Echelon" three times. Boy did that spark more interest. Damn right it did.

During the hours of my preparation for this book, and especially after Rooney became my focus, I learned that Rooney and I had covered some of the same ground in Europe—Liverpool, the Moors, and Bristol in England, and some areas of France, to name a few. The final item that caused me to focus on Rooney as one who might at the least have some knowledge of that infamous article was information regarding the request of one of the generals on General Eisenhower's Staff, the same officer who is credited with making the suggestion that Negro soldiers in segregated service units be given a chance to join White infantry units at the time of the Battle of the Bulge. Sometime before the invasion of France, General John C. H. Lee requested that the *Stars and Stripes* in London cover a ceremony of him giving an award to a Negro quartermaster supply sergeant for outstanding service. Rooney was given the assignment. He traveled the 20 miles or so to the site in South England. He wrote the story, but didn't use the term Negro or Black. The Editor allowed the article to be printed, but pictures were not included, resulting in another failed opportunity to show the involvement of Negroes in the war in Europe. Rooney was perhaps the last, best hope for resolving the mystery of the "Rear Echelon" ghost writers; that is, unless we can find a copy of that 1944 issue in someone's archives.

October came and some signs of fall began to show. The German Armies retreated a little, but battles raged, and the Red Ball Express kept on trucking. I don't recall seeing another copy of the *Stars and Stripes.* By this time I wasn't thinking much about that anymore. Whatever there was to think about regarding that matter was in the subconscious and would resurface in due time. By early November the weather began to cool and we changed to warmer uniforms. Advanced troops had already moved beyond Metz and were engaged in battles with some of Hitler's best panzer units.

Our side was winning those battles I know, to the dismay of the Fuhrer. The Ardennes became silent.

Suddenly it was December and the weather got colder in most areas of the region. Snow began to fall in many places, especially in the northern parts of France, Belgium, and Western Germany. The forward movement of Allied troops slowed down. Things got awfully quiet on the Western Front. Strong feelings abounded in these early days of December. There was very little movement anywhere. It was like everybody sensed that something big was going to happen. And, indeed, something big did happen. It was big and it was different. In the early days of a very cold winter the Germans launched a major counter offensive in the Ardennes of France and Belgium on December 16, 1944. Hitler had taken over command of his armed forces and designed an offense that, apparently, he thought would turn the tide in his favor. Hitler was losing the War. The Russian Army was giving him hell on the Eastern Front and the Allies on the Western Front were kicking his butt big time. Only the harsh weather conditions slowed the forward progress of our troops.

In organizing this massive attack in the Ardennes, Hitler moved some of his crack armored divisions from the

Chapter 3

Russian front. He selected his most trusted and dependable military leaders to lead the effort in the Ardennes. This included the fanatical Nazi General Zepp Dietrich, Commander of the crack 6th SS Panzer Army, Field Marshal Walter Mandel, General Alfred Jadel, and General Hoss Voce Mantener. A total of 31 German divisions; 6 artillery tank battalions and infantry hit American troops hard and opened a 60-mile-wide gap in the lines at Belgium, killing and wounding thousands of American soldiers, many of them just recently arrived from training camps in the United States. The Battle of the Bulge had begun.

A Dastardly Act

CHAPTER 4

THE GENERAL'S INVITATION AND THE BLACK SOLDIERS' RESPONSES

Sitting at a distance from the extreme danger, we wondered with anxiety what was really happening up front. Officers and the few others with military field phones had some sense of the big picture, but they were not sharing much, so the rest of us had to rely on our imaginations for a while. On Christmas Day 1944 the weather in our area was still damp and cold, but snow was not falling and our movement was not particularly restricted. That didn't provide any significant degree of relief. My mind was still in a bind. Every one of us had concerns. For a while after Dijon, my company occupied a building, which at some previous time might have been a manufacturing business of some sort before the Germans invaded France in 1940. It had many rooms of different configurations sufficient to store our equipment and allow movement of our people. Even our mess sergeant

and his staff had space to store their field utensils and C-
and K-rations, and still have room to move around. That
was an unusual convenience and nobody complained. And
on Christmas Day, in this little place somewhere between
Verdon and Metz, France, in the middle of a hot war, our
mess sergeant, the chef, whose name I don't remember,
served our command a freshly cooked, hot Christmas dinner
with all the trimmings. The turkey and dressing with giblet
gravy were very good and the pumpkin pie topped it all off.
We were totally surprised and I wondered how could they do
that? No K- or C-rations that day. The meal put everybody
in a pleasant state of mind, a state of mind that would last
for only a little while.

Shortly after the food was gone and we all had a
chance to say Merry Christmas, our company commander
came into the dining area with his head a little low. Someone
called attention and everything came to a halt. The room
that just moments earlier had been the scene of festivity,
was now stone quiet. The captain took out a single sheet
of paper. He made brief comments that, in effect, summed
up or confirmed what some of us had been thinking: the
Germans had indeed launched a major offensive along
American and British lines in Belgium, resulting in the death

of many American soldiers and infantry units in the area needed replacement. He further summarized a letter from Allied Commander General Dwight D. Eisenhower, which essentially invited Negro soldiers from segregated units in Europe to join ranks with White infantry units already on the front lines. "Every available weapon at our disposal must be brought to bear upon the enemy" to "deliver the knockout blow." The invitation indicated that the Negro soldiers would be treated fairly as comrades in arms to end hostilities. There would be no discrimination when these groups were assembled. More details would be provided by a 1st lieutenant of our company. The captain then said good luck and left the room.

The lieutenant stepped forward and spoke briefly. He explained the paperwork that each volunteer would be required to complete. He then moved to an adjunct room where volunteers could meet with him for a review of the details and completion of all paperwork. When the lieutenant left the room, there was a constant buzz, with guys talking seriously about this surprise invitation. While it was, in great sense surprising, this turn of events didn't really come to me as something totally out of the realm of reality. I am confident that each Black guy in that room

acknowledged that moment as one of the many first steps to change for our people that we all knew would come. What we didn't know was the precise circumstances in which such change would occur and for me, and us, was of little importance. What was, is, and always will be important, is that change comes and that I/we do everything necessary to promote it and support it—even approaching the face of death for the change we seek.

The moment the captain completed his speech and turned to leave the room I knew for certain what I was going to do. I didn't think twice about this offer, and when the Lieutenant opened his briefcase to offer documents for signature by the volunteers, I was among the first to step forward to receive and sign that paper to volunteer for front-line combat service for my country. The room was full because there were many who showed interest. I saw several from my platoon who signed the paper. One of them was that person whose voice I heard back in New York the night the 377th Engineering Battalion marched with pride and dignity toward the docks to board a ship to war while some dummy from a nearby segregated White company attempted to ruin our evening with his vile racist question.

Yes! That person who calmly put the dummy in his place, was a volunteer.

For hours after all the formal commitments were made, we sat around in small groups talking about the situation before us and reaffirming our commitment. I think we as a group had begun to feel a deeper kinship; we had something else in common that would bind us. As discussions continued, obvious thoughts of home surfaced. They lingered for a while, and then as quietly as they had surfaced they would disappear. Never for a moment did I see or hear of any questions or hint of doubt about any aspect of the issue.

We were aware of the dangers involved. We knew extremely bad weather had grounded most support for the divisions in the area. We knew also that the commander of Allied Forces had asked for help and had extended a formal invitation to us to join the action. We knew of the courageous action of Lieutenant General John C. H. Lee, an officer in General Eisenhower's command, who had the guts to suggest allowing Black soldiers from the segregated units in Europe to integrate the White infantry. And yes, we knew that our families and organizations back home wanted and were seeking on our behalf the best opportunity for us to

have success at the highest levels. And above all, we knew we could do it. And we could do it with class. All we needed was opportunity. As the remainder of the evening passed, I pulled away to the confines of my own thoughts. I didn't need any other encouraging words or wishes of good luck. I was ready to go.

The next day all of us who had stepped forward as volunteers were out of there. We were transported to a location some distance away where we met soldiers from the other all-Negro units. We were administered a series of tests, including physical and aptitude, and we passed with "flying colors" and stood ready for the next hurdle, whatever that might be. From there we were taken to a final processing center where our first test at integration occurred. Having arrived at this place early in the day, we were able to get through the screening by noon. Four of us and one White guy were assigned to a tent that held eight. We put our packs in designated places and started a conversation. Everything went well, no discernible problems. We had a few hours of free time before curfew and this group of five decided to check out the little town a few miles away. No one in authority said we couldn't, so we walked and talked.

Chapter 4

As we entered the town we could tell it had taken some hits as fighting moved through the area.

Further observation confirmed to us that this was not a cultural center. On selecting a place that looked safe enough, we had food and a drink and then left. On our return to camp after dark, we entered our tent and discovered that three other soldiers had been assigned there, giving us a full house. These guys were already asleep.

At daybreak the new guys woke us up with their chitchat and suddenly realized that they were in the company of four Negroes and one other White soldier. At that point one said to the others, "Come on now, let's act like White men." There was no more chitter-chatter from them. We had no need to respond and didn't. They quickly gathered their stuff and got out. We determined they were new guys, just from the States, coming in as replacements. I never saw them again. *Observation number 78.* Later that morning, following a light field ration breakfast, we learned that we were moving out to a training site in France where we would be engaged in intensive infantry training. When we arrived that afternoon it was cold with light snow. We were eager to get started. There were about 300 Negro

A Dastardly Act

O
P
Y

HEADQUARTERS
COMMUNICATIONS ZONE
EUROPEAN THEATER OF OPERATIONS

AG 322 x 353 XSGS

APO 887
26 December 1944

SUBJECT: Volunteers for Training and Assignment as Reinforcements.

TO: Commanding General, Southern Line of Communications.
Commanding General, United Kingdom Base.
Section Commanders, Communications Zone.

      1. The Supreme Commander desires to destroy the enemy forces and end hostilities in this theater without delay. Every available weapon at our disposal must be brought to bear upon the enemy. To this end the Theater Commander has directed the Communications Zone Commander to make the greatest possible use of limited service men within service units and to survey our entire organization in an effort to produce able bodied men for the front lines. This process of selection has been going on for some time but it is entirely possible that many men themselves, desiring to volunteer for front line service, may be able to point out methods in which they can be replaced in their present jobs. Consequently, Commanders of all grades will receive voluntary applications for transfer to the Infantry and forward them to higher authority with recommendations for appropriate type of replacement. This opportunity to volunteer will be extended to all soldiers without regard to color or race, but preference will normally be given to individuals who have had some basic training in Infantry. Normally, also, transfers will be limited to the grade of Private and Private First Class unless a noncommissioned officer requests a reduction.

      2. In the event that the number of suitable Negro volunteers exceeds the replacement needs of Negro combat units, these men will be suitable incorporated in other organizations so that their service and their fighting spirit may be efficiently utilized.

      3. This letter may be read confidentially to the troops and made available in Orderly Rooms. Every assistance must be promptly given qualified men who volunteer for this service.

JOHN C H LEE
Lieutenant General, U. S. Army
Commanding

Text of General David D. Eisenhower's Letter of December 1944, granting privilege to limited number of Colored troops to integrate combat units

50

soldiers in this group and for two weeks we trained hard and everything went well.

However, there were two incidents that stand out very clearly in my mind today. One of them involved what some thought might be enemy activity. In the courtyard of the three-story building where we lived while in training, there was a large barrel we used as a heater each morning while waiting for orders. We filled the barrel with wood or anything that would burn and it produced much heat. We made a circle around the barrel, sometimes two or three deep, taking turns to get closer to the heat. Early one morning after we had put scraps of wood on the coal left from the night before and the fire was going well, there was a large explosion in the barrel. Several guys were hit by shrapnel from the blast. The person in front of me was hit in both arms and blood was running all over him. Medics got there quickly and took care of the wounded. That was the end of the courtyard barrel fires.

The question for me was, what happened there? Two thoughts came quickly to mind—enemy sabotage or administrative training tactics. Whatever, it had an effect. No more assumptions; question everything and take care of business. We did and we got sharp!

A Dastardly Act

The second incident involved the shooting of one of the Negro soldiers by a White sentry at the entrance to the courtyard. On that day, while we were in the field training, administrators of the program placed two White sentries at the gate where there had never been a guard before. As we were returning from the training site miles away, we were stopped at the edge of the little town by our commander, who informed us of the shooting. The person who was shot was not on training assignment that day. He was returning from a nearby tavern after guards had been placed at the gate. According to officers, he was ordered to stop. He didn't and he was shot and killed on the spot. The commander pleaded for calm. Moments passed. There was no discussion among us at the time. We resumed formation and marched toward our headquarters, heads held high but spirits mixed. As we moved closer toward the gate of the courtyard the mood was tense. Two armed guards were in their designated positions. We walked through the gate two-by-two. No one spoke. The mood didn't change much for the remainder of that evening.

The next morning we were served hot coffee and donuts by two Negro USO staff. This didn't have much effect on us, but what did have an effect was the announcement that training was over and we were being assigned to combat units along the Belgian, German, and French borders. In no time our bags were packed and we were on our way. As we marched through the streets of this little French town on our way to board trucks for our journey to face Hitler's panzer units, locals lined both sides of the narrow streets to bid us farewell. We could hear their voices clearly in their best French, mostly women, old men, and some children saying, "Terminez la guerre! Terminez la guerre!"—Finish the War! Those words lingered for some time. The French had had enough. Thoughts of my high school social studies class kicked in. "It's my time now," I thought.

Several of the people I had gotten to know during this training period were assigned along with me to the 14th Armored Division. Douglas Daniels, the soldier from the 377th Engineers who responded quickly to the insensitive question in New York, was also with this group. We both were assigned to the 19th Armored Infantry Battalion of the 14th Division. While these administrative transactions were going on, I don't remember seeing or signing any document confirming our status in this division. At the time it didn't matter. Our country needed us and we were prepared for that. That was our attitude.

Volunteers were assigned to ten different combat divisions: the 1st, 2nd, 9th, 11th, 14th, 19th, 69th, 78th, 99th, and the 104th. These Divisions, as part of the overall Allied offensive in Europe, took the fight to the German Army in an aggressive plan that succeeded. Although we had become integrated as a combat unit, some issues probably did pose an essential challenge for the White officers having responsibility for organizing the first ever racially integrated military combat operation. Volunteers were required to give up their rank to participate, and no Negro soldier was placed in a position where he would give orders to any White soldier. One would expect the organizing White officers to acknowledge the numerous potential challenges the volunteers would face. While I can't confirm here with plan documentation what the planning officers expected, I suspect the general's office anticipated a positive response to his invitation and aggressive action in combat. And that's exactly what he got.

Thoughts or concerns like these were neither critical nor essential for us at these times. Succeed here and address concerns later. We soaked it all up and put it in our book of memories. We were there in the midst of a giant task force of tank battalions, field artillery, signal companies, cavalry, reconnaissance, ordinance, and other infantry. We felt pretty good.

The 14th Armored Division was moving east toward the City of Frankfurt, Germany. As we swept through this area, we could see the effect of the U.S. Army Air Corps' heavy bombing months prior to the invasion. Frankfurt, a highly industrial center and major player in Hitler's war machine, was obviously a major target of Allied Forces. Beyond Frankfurt, we turned southeast into the German State of Bavaria. Lots of American soldiers and airmen were released from German prisoner of war (POW) camps as we moved through these areas.

Once we reached Bavaria and moved past the city of Nuremberg, the forward thrust of our unit slowed somewhat. American airmen and soldiers were seen walking through the streets in small groups at a time as our armored units moved east. We had the German Army on the run (in retreat), then they would regroup and counterattack.

Nuremberg had been spared the heavy bombing and didn't suffer the same fate as Frankfurt. The educational and cultural institutions there were pretty much intact. It was an ideal place to conduct trials for higher ranking German officers of the Adolf Hitler regime after the war.

Late one afternoon, our armored column moved in single file along a narrow dirt road that led us over and around some small hills and toward what appeared, from a distance, to be medium dales, or valleys, when suddenly something different came into view. That something different began to look like an airport runway, except there were no buildings or other structures nearby. As we slowly proceeded along the narrow dirt road which seemed to be leading us a bit closer to the large expanse of concrete, somebody yelled "Autobahn, German Super-highway." It was big and quite intriguing, especially since we came upon it so suddenly. As it was a surprise to most of us, it was not a surprise to the reconnaissance (ReCon) group. It was their job to know where and what everything is. Nevertheless, it was an interesting sight. No vehicles were seen anywhere, and we wouldn't expect any, especially during the daylight hours. Perhaps at night, but that would be risky. All the intrigue ceased just as we approached a connecting road to an underpass toward the Autobahn. We were greeted with heavy rounds of mortar fire from an enemy mortar unit sitting at a distance, somewhere back in those partially wooded hills. We, the infantry quickly dismounted vehicles and took up defensive positions, prepared to fight, to kill.

There was no attempt to advance on us. We held our positions for a while, taking note of everything around us. We soon returned to our vehicles and moved a bit closer for a better view. All thoughts of the super highway by now were super gone. No way was it a factor in our minds.

The remaining daylight turned to darkness. Our tank units moved up to join the infantry and a line of defense was established. Some of our guys rode on tanks for most of the night to ensure that nothing penetrated our line. I think General Eisenhower would have been pleased with the level of mutual support. Kudos for integration.

Before daylight, the tanks pulled back to their previous positions as command seemed to assess the overall situation. What German units are here? And how many? Our platoon regrouped and prepared for the next orders. During the afternoon a decision was made to remove an obstacle in our path. The Germans had posted two of their big tanks on a wooded hill two or three miles ahead. The tanks were overlooking our advancing forces with presumed impunity. Our strategy was to move southward, out of view of their command position. We came upon a little farming community and spent the night there hashing out plans

and securing more weapons. The civilians had all moved out and we took over the farmhouses.

While some of the men provided security for the area, others who knew a little about cooking, went to the kitchen. By midnight, a hot meal of fried chicken, mashed potatoes, and biscuits were on the table. The brothers in the group had done themselves justice. Everybody had one biscuit and at least one piece of chicken. This was probably a case of "Victors' Rights" or "Might Is Right." Regardless, the farm family was not dealt any physical harm and our group managed to relax for a short while. The farmer could raise more chickens.

As I recall, I had second-shift security duty that night. It was already dark when I walked out to the security post about 10:00 p.m. and I could barely see the first-shift guy I was replacing while I walked toward him. The post was about 60 or 70 yards from the steps of the farmhouse we had accessed earlier in the day. As I approached, I gave the usual security word, which in this instance was a name or something like that. If there had been any peculiar issues related to security in that area, he would have informed me quickly. He returned to the house and I took a secure position close to the ground, making an effort to blend in with the environment. Nighttime, tall weeds and grass; it was not complicated. I got close to the ground by lying prone. This would give me the best chance to see any movement walking or crawling. Even from this position in the darkness of the night, it was difficult to see a man 10 or 15 feet away. In that situation my finger was always at the trigger. My two or three hour watch at the security post was uneventful—no Nazi or other messenger of the Fuhrer tried to breach our security that night. On my return to the farmhouse, I could still smell the fragrance of the country fried chicken that the brothers had prepared several hours earlier. A few of them were sitting around conversing about that delight. There was a jovial atmosphere in the house.

Before daybreak the next morning our mood had changed. At dawn, in full gear, with added firepower, we moved out of the little village on foot, moving first around our base camp, then up the hill to reach the wooded area. Then we climbed some more. At the top, about 60 yards away—Bingo! Two German tanks were sitting there in battle formation. The problem for them was, they were facing the wrong direction! We had come to their left flank. A few of their crew were standing outside their vehicles. When we opened fire, some made an effort to scramble back to their vehicles.

They were gallant, but not quite the match for what we had brought to the party. One tank was knocked out after a few minutes of fire and the other was damaged, but it could still fire some of its guns. It pulled back out of range of some of our weapons and tilted slightly causing its large gun to fire just over our heads. As we took a squatting position to fire on it, their smaller guns seemed to be functioning, too. I might have worked my way around the line of fire of the tank's guns to hit him with the 50-caliber, but the lieutenant called for artillery support. At a distance of about 60 or 70 yards from the crippled tank, we lay flat on the ground as artillery dropped in some rounds while searching for range. After a few rounds they had the target; issue settled with the tanks and their command post destroyed. On our way out of the woods, I saw Medics coming up the hill to take care of the wounded and fallen. I knew there would be many more days like this as the 14th pressed eastward and southeast.

By April the weather was pretty good. We couldn't always keep track of specific dates or tell Sunday from Monday, but that was not very significant. However, I do remember the date we received the news of the death of President Franklin D. Roosevelt. We were on the trail of a German Unit traveling along another backcountry road

President Franklin D. Roosevelt

when we suddenly came up to a steel bridge over the Danube River. The span of the bridge which had been blown up at its center was about 45 or 50 yards. It looked like the bridge had been damaged in haste as the enemy retreated to the other side. Our infantry platoon dismounted and took positions along the sheer bank looking for signs of the enemy while waiting for orders. The bridge is out; the enemy is on the other side. Thoughts of having to swim the Danube danced through my mind. Also on the other side of that river, beginning a few yards from the foot of the bridge, was another very small village, containing small shops, grocery stores, and a few barns. On the right edge of the village was a field about 150 yards long, a barn or two, and a few piles of hay, or something like that. We had a good view.

We scanned around the area for enemy soldiers across the river, as units of our tank battalion pulled up behind and joined in. We all were stretching our eyes for any sign of enemy presence. In a moment I noticed movement near one pile of hay. He stood and started running toward what appeared to be a gun placement. I put him in my rifle sight and fired some rounds. No more movement there. The tank near me fired some rounds into that area from its big gun. I saw no other activity in that field. Shortly thereafter

Chapter 4

we noticed a white flag ascending up from the river along a beam of the bridge and determined it to be a German soldier surrendering. We realized then that the bridge had not completely severed at the center. The platoon crossed the Danube, on that half-bombed out bridge, one soldier at a time, everyone covering another's back, until we all moved safely across. The platoon spread out to check every nook and cranny for German soldiers. My recollection is that only one turned up, the others had retreated farther back into their home turf, no doubt to effect a stronger defense. It was very likely that we or some other allied unit would see them again.

In the little village there was only one primary street and a couple of alleys. So when we left to return to our vehicles, we were confident there was nothing there to do our troops any harm. As I started walking back to the bridge from the far eastern edge of the village, I noticed one of our guys engaged in what appeared to be heated debate with a German woman. When I moved closer to the scene I learned that our guy was concerned about the contents of a large piece of luggage she was carrying. She was dragging the large bag across the street when she was asked to stop and open it. She defiantly refused. By this time I was a little

closer and I heard the soldier distinctly ask the woman to open the bag, which was lying on the ground in the middle of the street. He asked again. She replied "no" in English. He fired several rounds from his automatic weapon into the bag until it opened. The woman cried like a little child. I walked away before the bag was fully open and never learned what the contents were. This soldier saw something suspicious; he approached it, and eventually dealt with it. That's taking positive action.

Our search of that little village on the Danube was complete. Though nothing significant turned up, something could have, and I am comfortable with the belief that whatever that something might have been, the platoon would have handled it. Our backs were covered, too. Now, back across the river, we moved with deliberate speed to get to our vehicles to establish the forward thrust to destroy the Nazis.

While moving toward our vehicles, I noticed a tall general standing in a Jeep talking to one of our guys. I wondered who he was, but didn't dare tarry or look concerned as I passed about 30 yards away. I heard a few guesses. Some even said it was General George Patton. By this time we were all mounted and about to pull away when an officer came up with a little guy, a German soldier, who had gotten himself captured. I was given the responsibility for guarding him until he could be turned over to the appropriate guard unit. We put him in the back of a truck. I stood about four feet behind him so that I could see him and both sides of the trail as we moved forward. Several miles up the trail, we came under heavy artillery fire. In my attempt to secure the prisoner first and take a defensive position, I did a horizontal butt stroke to his head with my rifle. The little guy ducked and apparently fell to the ground or under the truck. In the fast pace of events, he disappeared. Had I shot him he would have been right there as we regrouped from that scrimmage. Instead, he was out of sight, but only for a little while. Other units coming behind us would pick him up for sure. We kept moving. And while we continued on our path to find and destroy, the sight of a General, Patton or not, so close to the action and so intimately involved was a continuing source of inspiration.

Inspirational Recall

After I began to write this account of my military experiences I discovered that there were many things I wanted to say and to include them in this memoir. I found it amazing inasmuch as I have spoken about my

General George Smith Patton Jr.,
Commander of the Third Army

time in the Army over the many years since I served in World War II, I hardly ever spoke of anything related to my actual involvement. It's quite refreshing that so much has come readily to my mind as I began to write. And what is so astonishing about it, is that it comes without effort. Like, I don't snap my fingers and say, "Here, now!" I call it inspirational recall. I really have felt some of the highs and lows of the actual experiences I had.

One of those occurred at about dusk one evening following a 12-hour fight for a German stronghold in the city of Bad Kissingen. It started before dawn on the northwestern edge of town where we had pulled up the night before for briefing and orders. Our reconnaissance team had stalked out an area of mostly single-family homes and other medium level buildings on the outskirts of Bad Kissingen from which to launch a ground attack. Under the cover of heavy artillery fire, we worked our way on foot through nearby roads, across a bombed railway station, and on to the streets of the city of Bad Kissingen. In some instances we made door-to-door checks as we moved forward if something looked suspicious. Something did look suspicious at one detached house as I rushed along the sidewalk near the house. I ran two or three paces to the house, hitting the doorknob hard

with the butt of my rifle, jarring the door wide open and I stepped inside four or five paces. In an instant there were a half-dozen guys on my heels. We were in the living room of a neat, very colorful, home. Seeing no signs of danger, I noticed a stairway that descended to what appeared to be a basement. I made two quick steps down, finger on the trigger, and then a baby cried. The baby's cries came as in a plea for mercy. Seeing no sign of a combatant I turned, the guys behind me turned, and we hit the street again moving forward with the rest of the platoon.

We moved toward to what appeared to be a bridge or overpass. I couldn't get the best view as I and several others took position along a street about a half-block away from the entrance to the bridge. We covered the left flank as our artillery constantly pounded the German forces ahead of us while we searched the streets and checked some apartments. While checking one apartment, we heard the house phone ring. It rang for a minute or more. No one answered. Seconds after the phone stopped ringing, a German tank or artillery fired their notorious gun at the apartment. It was a direct hit at the ceiling of that apartment. We hit the floor hard. We could hear the phone ringing in apartments adjacent, one apartment at a time, and following each ring, we could hear an incoming projectile, a distinct sound, a direct hit. It seemed that the Germans had placed their infamous 88mm anti-tank at a level that enabled them to fire the "88s" horizontally for a direct hit on the building. We managed to escape that situation unharmed. They knew we were in the area and they tried hard to take us out. I like to think that the peculiar sound of that big projectile while in flight aided in our efforts to quickly find the lowest spot on the ground. I call that the 3-second notice.

After spending hours in the adjacent streets surrounding the bridge entrance that the Germans strongly defended, I noticed that we had, in fact, sustained some injuries. How many, I didn't know, but the Germans suffered more than we. The sun never came out that day. Heavy overcast was constant and at about dusk, after 12 hours in that rather confined area, I noticed what appeared to be a phased withdrawal as the number in my squad on the street had declined. While I had not gotten word of any scheduled movement, I made an assumption that change was ordered. The banging was continuous from the 14th Division Artillery as it pumped rounds at the German position like it was now or never. I would like to say it was

music to my ears, but honestly that was not the case. Bombardment was unrelenting and I felt good about it.

As I was one of the last guys in my group to leave the street we were covering, I noticed a person had been shot one street over. I was hoping the guys on the street near him had rescued him as they left the area. Things had been happening fast all around. Sniper fire was apparent. One American I saw on the ground was on his back with one leg propped up and his rifle lying beside him. Nobody else was very close to him at the time. I didn't get back to that side of the street as I was engaged with things more directly to my left, a half block away. At times, the sound of your own heavy weapon can be daunting.

I learned that a fresh platoon was in the process of replacing us and was concerned about the dwindling number of comrades in the area. I moved fast to an intersection and did a quick pivot and saw squads from another platoon heading in my direction. They were moving quietly, with deliberate speed, and a look of determination. I understood the drill and made a move of my own. I did an about face to check the street I had been occupying for hours. The street was empty and the building still standing, mostly. And the people—those who occupied this space when war was not being waged—were there, deep into the basements of every building in the city, filling every space available and then some. And the enemy? He was there, just beyond that embankment and beyond that wall, not willing to accept yet that it was his time to die. He had a choice. He could drop his arms and raise a white flag or accept the consequence of being on the wrong side. These were my thoughts.

Feeling reasonably certain that I would be okay, I turned back to face the replacement squads. They were within speaking range, and before I could wave my hand at the lead soldier, heavy volleys of artillery erupted. I hit the ground quickly. He understood what the experience might have been like earlier just a few short blocks away. As we passed close by, he reminded me that the heavy ones I just heard and the continuing ones were from our side, taking it to the enemy. Of course, I knew that, but I didn't hurt myself either by hitting the dirt a few times while racing to catch up with my platoon, which by this time had arrived back at the rendezvous site.

Daylight turned to darkness again and within a short time I had retraced my steps of the early morning. I joined my group and listened for a while to the conversation. That session broke up and smaller groups formed to compare

notes regarding experiences of the day. I sat alone, acknowledging my blessings. Later we had a meal of field rations (C or K) and dropped off to sleep. Little did it matter that we were in the midst of conflict. We were confident that while we were getting rest, someone covered our backs.

At dawn the next day, we mounted vehicles and headed out for the next target. "Mounted?" one might ask. "You bet," said I. That's reality in an armored infantry battalion. Quickly, we kissed Bad Kissingen goodbye, with no thought of ever seeing her again, although we could have. Word came later that the city had fallen. Some days later, my platoon was ordered to take time out for R&R. We were away from the front lines for a couple of days where a hot shower and a hot meal were available. During this short time away, I had hoped to see a current issue of the *Stars and Stripes,* but none was available. We were provided a new set of clothes, which we welcomed with open arms.

On our return to the front, reestablishing our place in forward movement was important to us. It appeared we were headed in the general direction of Munich, the city where Hitler had started gaining his power. We were traveling in an area where the hilly terrain enabled us to see parts of our column in front for nearly a mile at times.

Awesome! Another day, the Allied air forces flew a bombing mission directly over our unit. These were a variety of types of bombers and they had fighter planes escorts. There were so many planes that they cast a huge shadow over our column for ten minutes or more as they passed over our heads. They were taking it to the Nazis. And if that was not a sight to behold, what we came up on later that day would certainly qualify.

Our unit came to a halt along a ridge overlooking a shallow valley where we watched two U.S. fighter planes, Mustang P-51s, attacking a German stronghold about a mile ahead of us. There was a group of buildings situated among clusters of pine trees. The pilots took turns dropping bombs at first, then one plane was hit by anti-aircraft fire from the German compound and went down. The pilot bailed out, his parachute opened, and he descended toward the ground, but just before he reached the level of the top of the trees, we heard gun fire from the ground. The Germans didn't have the guts to take him prisoner.

We were on our toes waiting for the order to go. When the plane went down, the other one momentarily disappeared, but he didn't go away. Seconds after his buddy was gunned down while floating to the ground in his

A Dastardly Act

parachute, the second pilot came out of the sky with the sun at his back and all guns firing. He released a bomb before coming out of the dive and when he was out of the dive, all guns on the ground were silent. As our column moved ahead I was hoping our platoon would get the assignment to check that area out, just in case there were some bad asses around who, by chance, might have escaped their just rewards. We didn't get that task, but I felt certain that the platoon assigned to that area had no problem remembering what happened to the pilot who had parachuted safely only to be gunned down at tree top.

We had read and heard a lot about German concentration camps. The most talked about and most notorious of them all was Auschwitz in Southwest Poland that was opened by the Germans in 1940 with 728 Polish Jews. Dachau was the second largest concentration camp in Europe. This camp was in southeast Germany, not far from Munich, and had actually been opened by Hitler in 1933 for political prisoners only two months after he came to power. Our unit was headed in that direction. The German Army was still fighting on all fronts, although Allied Forces had inflicted some serious pain on Adolf's warriors. News came that the Russians were closing hard in their move from the northeast toward Berlin, which was good news. We kept pushing on.

Suddenly, in May, full German battalions started surrendering. One morning as my unit advanced slowly along a narrow two-lane road, the column stopped. Looking to our right, high upon a ridge about two hundred yards away, we could see white flags waving. First, there was one flag, then three, six, and in a matter of seconds, a long line of German soldiers emerged from the high brush on the ridge. It seemed that a whole army was surrendering. Within ten minutes they all were out of the brush, moving downhill slowly in formation. They had laid down their arms before the first flag appeared. The appropriate division officers went out to meet them and take them prisoner. Our column remained in place, ready for any necessary action, but to be sure, nothing sinister was about to happen among that band of enemy soldiers (approximately 1,000); they were ready to quit. Military police were very likely headed to the scene to take charge of them.

In a short while our column moved on ahead to "Finish the War," as the people of that small village back in France—old men, women, and young children—had implored us to do. Every hour it became increasingly clear

that the German Army was unequivocally ready to quit. And quit they did. On all battlefields German soldiers began to lay down their weapons. That included Hitler's best, the crack infantry units and panzer divisions. And, yes, the fanatics who helped to breach Allied defenses in Belgium, in December 1944 put down their guns. At this point on this day, for all practical purposes, the war in Europe was over. The official word came to us shortly after unconditional surrender by the German Army was completed, June 7, 1945, in Reims, France. On that day my unit was moving closer and closer to Munich. The German concentration camp, Dachau, was nearby. By October, the camp would be holding German officers pending trial for their atrocities. So very much was happening in the European Theater of Operations. History was in the making and there we were, in the midst of it. We had learned of Hitler's death in his bunker earlier and acknowledged the potential of "the other shoe to drop"—we thought of the Pacific Theatre and the idea that possibly others would follow Hitler's lead.

With the critical danger in Europe over, we could take a little time out to focus on issues beyond our immediate environment. We could look more closely at things around us and think more intellectually about our presence and our purpose. And we could begin to think, to some extent, about our future. Most importantly, we could take some time to think about home. There was minimal communication between the battlefield and home during the period of June 1944-June 1945, and while home was always a breath away, even during the toughest of times, it was never practical to allow thought of home to interfere with the soldiers' business on the battlefield. Any good soldier would corroborate that statement.

Among the many thoughts that circulated through my mind during the immediate period following the German surrender was the letter from General Eisenhower's office that my engineering unit received on Christmas Day, 1944, which essentially said, "Help needed, you are invited." On hearing that call for support from the general, I felt impressed. It set in motion a perspective I needed, and I suspect that was true for each of the 5,000 volunteers from segregated service units. I knew instantly I would step up to the plate in response to that invitation. My act of saying, "Yea, I'll go," reflected more than the depth of my patriotism; it reflected the quality of my spirit in efforts to accomplish what is right, fair and just, for me, my people—any people and all people. Then, looking back in that moment, and that brief

act, I felt good, proud that I had stepped forward. Someone asked, "Would you do it again?" and my response would be, "I am confident I would do it again." Those few moments of reflection were good for me. That question of participation would come sooner or later. The enemy's surrender in June evoked a response sooner. A good exercise for my mind.

General Dwight D. Eisenhower,
Supreme Commander of the Allied Expeditionary Forces

A Dastardly Act

CHAPTER 5

WAR'S END AND RECONCILIATION

At the time of Nazis surrender we were in the German State of Bavaria, still moving in the general direction of the City of Munich. When the forward movement stopped, the various companies and platoons were assigned shelter in the different cities, towns, and villages in the area. My platoon was assigned shelter in the small town of Haag, located about 18 miles west of Munich. The Dachau Concentration Camp was just a few miles north of Haag. We were housed in a building that might have been the site of a food processing business and occupied this facility for about two months as our platoon headquarters. It was not in the best of shape, but that didn't affect us in a negative way. It had walls and a ceiling that was adequate enough. In Haag there were three or four local sites where German prisoners were kept. Some were being held for investigation and/or trial. Members of our platoon were called on to provide security while these guys were

held captive. The task was light, not demanding, and did not consume an inordinate amount of time. This provided ample opportunity for us to see another side of German—to meet, observe, and chat with the German civilians—men, women, and children, even families—if any were inclined to talk. We would have another perspective of this large country that was so completely consumed by the powerful will of the Fuhrer. Conversations with the locals would enhance our efforts to learn more about the area and the character of the people. There was a small German hospital nearby that housed some German officers and enlisted soldiers. A few civilians might have received medical help there as well. American military doctors also worked out of this small hospital, providing medical services to U.S. Service members. All were White.

The only medical assistance I sought while in Germany was at this little hospital at the village of Haag. When I walked into the doctor's office and explained the pain in my shoulder, he looked confused and left the room without a comment. I thought ten minutes was a long enough time to wait and I left the room. I didn't report the incident to my company commander or to anyone; perhaps I should have reported it, but I didn't. I made a note of it though. "No big deal, one might say! Yuck, but they do add up."

Another site where German prisoners were held was situated on the outskirts of Haag. It was a huge, cage-type structure with partial see-through walls similar to cages that house circus animals. Individual prisoners were kept separate in these contraptions, which appeared strong and secure. A guard was posted on the grounds outside the facility where he had full view of the prisoners at all times, and of course, the prisoners had full view of the guard. I had sentry duty at this location once or twice and it was a bit creepy. There was one prisoner I had responsibility for guarding for a two-hour period one evening who might have fit the description of the "fanatical Nazi," General Sepp Dietrich, commander of the crack German 6th Panzer Army, one of the five or six top German officers in the Ardennes of Belgium and France in December 1944. He did look wild and very strange. He moved around in his "cage" as if he were in command of those surrounding him. When I took that post I didn't ask questions about the occupant and I don't recall anyone calling this one by a specific name. However, as I made my pass around that facility, my finger was always near the trigger. The chances of something going astray at

the time were slim; still I remembered the incident back in Dijon, France. "The Gestapo might attempt anything," I reasoned, even in defeat. Those tasks were light and at times fascinating, but they were always about taking care of business. It didn't take much effort to remember that.

Some of our group went into the concentration camp at Dachau to check out the deplorable conditions there. This camp was almost as notorious for its cruelty and treatment of Jews as Auschwitz in Poland. Functioning at maximum capacity, Dachau housed thousands of people. It also confined others not related to the crime of being a Jew, such as Russian prisoners of war, political prisoners, priests, and others Hitler considered unfit for the "New Germany." Our guys who went into Dachau were horrified at the sight of so much inhumanity. Just the thought of what went on there aroused anger, especially contemplating that just some weeks earlier this place was within our ability to liberate.

I did go into Munich and, no doubt, walked some of the streets that Hitler walked during his lifetime. While I didn't get to the beer hall, I did visit Munich sites. All of this, of course, was after the fighting forces of the Fuhrer decided to quit. While walking along those streets of Munich, I walked with a feeling of triumph over evil, triumph over a man with an extraordinarily evil personality. I thought a lot about many things: the various concentration camps scattered about Germany and neighboring countries the German leader had annexed for his own gratification; Jesse Owens' success winning four gold medals in the 1936 Olympics in Berlin and how Owens' success infuriated Hitler so much that he left the arena early to avoid greeting Owens with congratulatory words (but he wasn't invited to the White House to shake hands with President Roosevelt either); and Max Schmeling, the big German heavyweight boxer, who had returned to the United States in 1938 for a second match with Black American pride and joy, Joe Louis, Heavyweight Champion of the World, to be knocked out in the first round. With that K.O., the Brown Bomber put an end to any thought the German fighter and his country's leader had about White supremacy in the ring. That was not going to happen.

I thought about how Hitler had ruled the lands from the Russian border to the English Channel and Atlantic Ocean, and how desperate the British were at Dunkirk in May of 1940 in their efforts to escape the onslaught of a rampaging German Army that had perfected the blitzkrieg as an art form. "Damn you, Hitler," I said in a tone reflecting

emotions rarely shown. Then suddenly another voice spoke, "Hey Brodus, the war is over." "Yeah," said I.

Our tour of Munich continued, but there was something else that kept flashing through my mind. It was the voice of my high school social studies teacher. She and the other teachers generally kept us aware of what was happening in Europe during those early years of WWII. I couldn't thank them enough for that. As I spoke with some of the German people on the streets and at local businesses, I listened carefully to what they had to say and how they responded to questions posed by guys in my group. It was kind of unreal to see those people so calm and simply moving slowly about, taking care of just small things, only weeks after having been relieved of the character who dominated their lives as if he owned them. Of course they knew their situation better than I. For some, there might have been an appreciable level of comfort with the way things were under that character. But, for so many others, I suspect that was not the case. In view of the many factors impacting the lives of the people on the streets of Munich at the time, it seemed that they were handling their situation pretty well, a step at a time.

Back in Haag we performed our chores with aplomb. Individuals within our group began to have conversations with German residents in the area. It was a little slow getting started, civilians and military talking. We were okay with that; we understood that some Germans might have been afraid to talk with African American soldiers. Some people in the area seemed to emerge from various hiding places as time passed. They would gradually appear at the windows of their homes and in their yards. Some would venture out onto the narrow streets of the little village. Increasingly, as we moved about taking care of our business, civilians began to initiate conversation by making eye contact or simply with a "Hello" or "Good morning." Some would just show up in a place where they could be spoken to. I think that most of the German civilians in the area were unsure about the correctness of speaking with the African American soldiers and our group didn't show any great haste to make their acquaintance.

The opportunity for me to meet a German family came one day when I returned to our building from duty at one of the sites where prisoners were being held. As I walked toward the door, I noticed a slender German youth about age 12 or 13 standing in the yard, 10 or 12 feet from

the door of the building. He looked as if he wanted to speak, but was not sure it would be all right to do so. I looked him in the eye and said, "Hello," not knowing what kind of response I would get, and to my surprise, he said "Hello" in distinct English. It was a pleasant surprise. I asked, "How are you?" and his response was, "I am fine." With that initial introduction, even though it was not really an introduction as I had not asked him his name and did not give him mine, I felt our basis was established for future conversation. I immediately recalled having seen the kid in that general area once before. I hadn't noticed anyone talking to him. He was just there, waiting for someone to say hello. I did and this young German boy seemed pleased with that.

For the time our platoon had first occupied this building, which we thought had been a food processing facility, there were boxes of dehydrated food products stacked on the ground in a corner just a few feet away from the entrance. Nobody in our group made use of them, they were just there. While the kid and I talked, I thought he might have an interest in the food packages that lay on the ground, so I asked him about his family. While I don't recall precisely what his response was, the indication was that he had one. The more we talked, the more impressed I became with his ability to speak English so well. I asked where he learned to speak English. "In school," he said. By this time I had made an assessment that this was a very bright young man. He was courteous and very polite, and I believe he addressed me as sir. I was encouraged to continue our conversation. While we talked I noticed him observing the packets of dehydrated food and I asked if he would like to have a bag of rice or beans. When he said "yes," I picked up a 5-lb. bag of rice and gave it to him. He thanked me and immediately left the area.

Several days passed before I saw the kid again. He showed up one afternoon, a few hours following my return from another assignment. It seems that he knew my schedule. As before, he came into the yard where I and a few of my platoon members were sitting around, just relaxing. When he spoke, he delivered a message from his parents: "Thank you for the bag of rice," they said. I acknowledged the parents' message in a manner that might be encouraging to them, realizing their son would very likely take back my response verbatim. I did that on purpose because I had already reached some conclusions about the kid and his family, although I had never met them. He stayed around for a while, simply observing these American soldiers, and seemingly pleased to be in their company. I wondered if his interest and apparent comfort level was caused by the fact that we were African Americans. If so, mark up one for the brothers. If not, there were no problematic issues here. When the young man gave a little signal that he was leaving I picked up a 5-lb. bag of butter beans from the little pile in the corner and handed it to him. He took the bag with a smile and quietly left the yard.

German youth who received bag of beans

Left to Right: Youth who received a 5-lb. bag of beans and his sister and brother at an earlier age.

During the short period of time since I first noticed this young German boy hanging around our headquarters, I had wondered more about the German people who had had no service-connected responsibilities with the Nazi regime. We knew something about the established German families who were considered among Hitler's prime citizenry and/or families of the high-ranking German officer corps and their privileges and obligations. Also we had known far too long and from so many sources about the plight of the Jewish population in Germany and the many other countries in

A Dastardly Act

Eastern Europe under Nazi control. Further, we were aware of conditions and lifestyles of so many others who seemed to have accepted Hitler's personality and domineering power because he regained territory that had been taken from Germany following WWI and because he built large factories all over Germany and gave people jobs from the early 1930s through 1943. Many German people accumulated wealth, bought beautiful homes, and lived what some would call a good life. So, whenever I saw a German civilian, whether up close or from a distance, I wondered which of these groups or classes did he or she represent? Someone asked, "Why do you raise these questions now? The war is over." I said, "But I am here in the midst of all that's left and these are things I'd like to know, especially about people in my presence." There was this German kid in our presence, and I felt certain I could get some answers to some of my concerns by observing and talking with him and eventually his parents and, conceivably, their neighbors. I reasoned that a smart kid didn't just get to be that smart all by himself. Chances are he had some help along the way.

On still another day my little friend from the neighborhood dropped by. This time he had exceptional news. He came to tell me that his parents would like to meet me. Of course I was interested in meeting the parents of this kid, so interested that I asked, "When? When can I meet them?" He said "Today," and I said, "I'm available today." I had no other responsibilities that evening and I was free to go.

Although the war was over, I was mindful that I was in a country whose leader we just defeated who had managed to convert a lot of followers during his reign of terror, and that some of them included members of the Gestapo who might very well be in hiding, even in the small village of Haag. That considered, I armed myself appropriately, then I was ready to go and we took to the streets, walking in the middle of the narrow street. There were no sidewalks. I felt comfortable in the streets. We walked with a moderate pace for me to be introduced to this intriguing family who had the audacity to invite me into their home. We walked several blocks and turned right into a courtyard about 400 feet long and 100 feet wide, with apartments lining both sides. The boy led the way to a ground level apartment on the left and opened the front door. Sitting in the living room was a neatly dressed family. The mother, father, a brother younger than my friend, and a teenage sister about 15. I was introduced to the family by the name of Bob, an assumed

A Dastardly Act

name for practical purposes. I was given the names of each family member, whose names I didn't record at the time, but when looking at a document, I could pick them out of a photo lineup of a dozen people, even today if there was a need to do so.

As I was being introduced, the family smiled as if they were greeting a friend they hadn't seen for a while. Using a mixture of English and German they extended pleasant greetings and welcomed me to their home. The son served as interpreter for most of our conversation. The mother did most of the speaking for the family, while the father confirmed her comments, and the two other siblings smiled showing their approval. I really got the impression they dressed up for the occasion. I had no problem with that, as the dress was casual. The father's proficiency in English seemed to be somewhat less than that of his wife. I remembered a few German words and phrases I had learned in England while preparing for D-Day, and to some extent they were helpful.

During the introduction and the conversation that followed, we remained in the living room of this relatively small apartment. We spoke briefly about my family. They were interested in knowing how they were doing, etc. As we talked, I was observing everything in sight. I recall that the mother appeared to be a bit frail. She had a slight cough, but her spirit was up, and she had confidence in her son. It was very clear that she trusted his initiative. The father, a short man, didn't appear to be very robust, but the younger brother and sister seemed to be in reasonably good health. There was no indication of wealth. This fact would seem to apply to most of the people in the village.

While I visited with this family, none of their neighbors knocked on their door to make an inquiry about anything, although the few who were in view when I arrived at the site did observe my presence with casual stares. I don't recall anyone speaking to the kid as we approached the area. Also, I was not introduced to any of this family's neighbors. For all the things I didn't see, I concluded that this was one confident, competent, courageous family. It seemed to me that my presence and my attitude toward them gave them a lift of some sort. As for the bag of questions in my mind going into that household, I left with a feeling that the German leader, Adolph Hitler, never came close to winning the heart and soul of this family. In fact, I suspect everything he did was counter to their principles and beliefs. And furthermore, I believe these people suffered more than the expressions on

their faces conveyed, or the implications of their interest in seeking the friendship of a Black guy from America.

My second visit to the home of this German family occurred a few days after my platoon (the volunteers from those segregated units) received orders to prepare for return to the United States. Of course that was good news for us, although it came somewhat suddenly. It meant a change of pace and we stepped up to it. It also meant that I would be seeing my recently acquired new friends sooner than anticipated. So, when I informed the young man that we would be leaving the area soon, he was anxious to have me bid his family goodbye. I arrived at the home in mid-afternoon and greeted everyone in the customary manner. I explained that I would be leaving their village and country within a few days and thanked them for their hospitality. We had a good round of discussion about my family. I shared a few photographs of relatives I had in my wallet of which they viewed carefully and made complimentary remarks. While the kid did the usual interpretation of phrases his parents couldn't say in English, they seemed to enjoy the experience anyway. At one point it seems that the mother tried to describe the appearance of one of my sisters in the photo she held in her hand. While she may have had

Chapter 5

difficulty with the description, I had no problem with it at all. The term was "Smooth Black." My sister would have accepted that as well. However, I don't recall telling her about that phrase.

During this extended conversation, all of the family members brought out some of their family photos and offered me copies to take with me. I accepted those photos with thanks. We continued our conversation while moving to about the center of the courtyard and from that position I had a good view of everything around me, even the windows of all the apartments around the courtyard. As I searched for another photo, I glanced around and noticed a woman and a man at the window on the third floor staring intently at the activity at the center court. Their ears were pressed to the window as if they were trying to hear our conversation. The expressions on their faces seemed to be filled with contempt. On viewing their stance, I raised my rifle with the barrel pointed in their general direction and they did a quick get away from the window. My glance at other windows or doorways in that building revealed nothing. I had noticed the woman in the third floor window on my first visit there. At that time she moved quickly away when she saw my weapon exposed. The people in that third floor

window clearly had some concerns. Their concerns were not just ordinary concerns, as their intense expressions suggested a variety of things. The American Soldier with the gun might be investigating some issue, like German Army officers who had committed crimes while enforcing Hitler's will. Or, on seeing the smiles and pleasant manner of the family with the American soldier, the couple in that window might have perceived this to be a very desirable contact to be envied. Any number of conditions might have applied here. I made no report of this observation because it was one of many possibilities that arose during the course of a week or a day that may or may not have substance under the existing circumstances.

We completed our exchange of information there on the courtyard, perhaps under the curious and watchful eyes of other locals, wondering from a distance what it was all about. I knew they were there. There was no danger and, as for my family of friends, I was reasonably confident they could handle their own situation. I shook their hands, wished them well, then turned and walked away. It did seem a little sad though. They were a bit special. Picking up my bag as I headed down the street, thoughts lingering, I determined that there were many other families throughout that country who, at that time, could have benefited in some small way from a conversation that reflected concern. From the first day of meeting the Haag family I wondered about their life under Nazi rule. I wondered if they were Jews. I didn't ask. Still don't know. Had my platoon remained in the village longer, I would have gotten answers to the bag of questions I had assembled in the back of my mind.

On return to my quarters following a short, brisk walk I put the Haag family address and pictures away and eased into a little meditation time about our scheduled journey back home. First thing up—the people of Germany. Not the military kind or the politicos. Our Allies' plan for them had already been decided before the war ended. The thoughts continuously circling my mind were about, perhaps, a majority of the German citizens who had had no vested interest in Hitler's war. For months now, I had been among many of them. Many suffered in some form or the other. Some more than others. Some had spoken, others had not. A few questions had been raised about life in America. Yeah! Recalling such questions and issues like the New York episode when we were boarding out ship quickly put my heart to flutter and brought an end to that attempt at meditation. And then, realities of the day took

their rightful place. We had just received notice that our group (the volunteers) would return to the United States where they would be given leave for a number of days. At that point that was the most we knew about our status in the 14th Armored Division.

When we volunteered for combat service with infantry units in December 1944 there was no mention of a future for us in the military beyond the end of "hostilities." None in our group had any idea of what was in store for us or what task, duty, or assignment we would be given when the war ended. What we did know was the Supreme Allied Commander, Dwight Eisenhower, called for support. He opened the door to integration of the military and we stepped in. There was no time to waste. No time to give in-depth thought about the issue of segregation in the Army of the United States of America. But, while we didn't have time to ponder the future, we did have hope and expectations. And I suspect every one of the generals in Eisenhower's office understood that. They understood, too, that we expected change beyond the date of the end of hostilities in Europe. Each one of those 2,221 Negro soldiers from the segregated units who was accepted in the Allied Commander's plans to "destroy the enemy forces and end hostilities" had a right to expect improved opportunities in a non-segregated U.S. military at the end of the war. At the least we expected distinct signs of progress toward that end.

Since the war ended, no officer had said anything remotely related to the future of the volunteers from the segregated Army units, nor had anyone from the government or anyone from the general's office raised any questions of us regarding the integration experience or our expectations for the future. So the order returning us stateside and the apparent breakup of the platoon caused me to contemplate, retrospectively. Since hostilities, I saw fewer of the White officers and NCOs in our area. Reflecting back to a short time before the war ended and German units were still resisting while we as a unit were still beating them down, the 14th Division Commander came to speak to the platoon one day. Fighting had really slowed at this point, so most of us gathered outside a big barn on a sprawling hillside farm to hear what the general had to say. He came with some kind of pep talk, complimenting us for our combat skills, etc. He said he would tell General B. O. Davis, Sr. about us. It is critical to note here that Davis was the only Black general in the U.S. military. There was no Black in the Navy or Marine Corps with a rank as high as general, a

sad commentary indeed. I understood the appropriateness of the reference to Davis. The general completed his speech and then left. I thought we might see the commander again, but it didn't happen. I wondered about that.

About ten minutes after the general left the area, a combat incident occurred that might have been of equal interest to him. A German pilot whom we later determined had concealed a biplane in one of the numerous barns on the farm, tried to escape in the plane. As we were shifting around reflecting on the general's presence and comments, there was the sudden sound of a motor starting. The sound was like a motorcycle. We all looked over to our left, about 300 yards away. Somebody said, "What the hell?" and we all took off, headed in the direction of the field and, in full view, the little plane became airborne. He had no chance. At about 1,500 feet, our division's artillery brought him down in seconds. The plane fell less than 200 yards from where the general was standing while making his speech. We reached the scene immediately. Obviously the pilot was dead. His spleen had probably burst because his body had swollen so quickly. Afterward, a search of the area revealed no other potential problems for us.

Reflecting further on issues related to our status while we were still in this area of the escape attempt I called the Big Farm Community, I noticed a number of little things that when viewed together would cause concern for most people. While the division commander spoke to us a few minutes before the attempted biplane escape, as he congratulated us for our fighting spirit, he concluded with one statement: "You've got to leave the women alone." I was never sure what that comment meant, but later that evening I noticed a White officer, a lieutenant, apparently chaperoning a German farm woman while she milked her cows inside a large barn. As I walked into the barn, I saw the woman laboriously milking one cow while several of my Black comrades sat on stools, wood rails, and stalls nearby, watching her perform her chores. The lieutenant was standing on a platform at a level a few feet above the soldiers and the woman, positioned to have a clear view of everyone in the area. As I moved a bit closer I heard some words exchanged between the Negro soldiers and the White officer, which sounded to be frictional. I wondered what had transpired there prior to my entrance. The woman didn't seem to be bothered. She continued hand milking the animal that seemed very content. The cow's bag was full

and it looked heavy with streams of milk coming down with each up and down movement of the farm woman's hands. I got the impression that she had a lot of experience milking cows. She kept milking. What a relief it must have been for that cow. The lieutenant didn't talk much; he just watched. After a while the substance of these reflective incidences began to shape my perspective of the things happening around us. It was now early July and it had become more than evident our service in the 14th and in Europe had come to an end.

CHAPTER 6

A BITTERSWEET RETURN TO HOME

The initial group of Negro combat infantry veterans was, as a matter of fact, processed out of the division and placed in a category for return to the United States. Yes, the thought of returning home to family and friends was very welcome news, but "Now tell me more," I reasoned, but no other information came. We began to prepare our minds for the trip back home. In my letters home to family regarding the good news, I didn't comment on any negatives. When travel orders arrived, we were completely ready. We were transported by military trucks to the nearest operating train station from which we would head for Belgium. It was amazing to see trains up and running so early after the war's end as Allied bombers did a job on enemy rail lines during the course of hostilities. New lines were repaired and smooth running trains were available for us. Once we were aboard, Germany was in our rear-view mirror. The route from Europe on

return to the States was a scenic one that took the long way round, through fantastic, out-of-the-way places. There were some of which we had seen before, but under different circumstances. One might say "this was better." It certainly was not complicated. It gave us the opportunity to see some places under bright lights, whereas 12 or 14 weeks earlier they were under siege in darkness.

Upon our arrival in Belgium every railway station was a gentle reminder of some historic event from the past. And the beautiful little port city of Antwerp was an ideal first stop on our journey home. Recalling the morning of our arrival in Antwerp, everything seemed calm with hazy sunshine, a gentle breeze, and practically no noise, the beginning of a wonderful day. Even the ease in which the train pulled into the station seemed choreographed, and stepping off the train, taking a breath of fresh Belgium air while observing the few people out and about was all very soothing. Everything in view—the trees, blooming flowers, and green shrubbery—all helped to make a beautiful scene and established, that day, a very real sense of peace in Antwerp, a condition quite the opposite from that of most Belgium communities just seven or eight months earlier— Leipzig and Bastogne were the epitome of "hell" back then. Although our time in Antwerp was relatively short, it certainly was an ideal first stop coming out of Germany.

After Antwerp we were taken to Brussels, Belgium, the place where General Dwight Eisenhower, as Supreme Allied Commander in Europe during WWII, established his headquarters following the D-Day invasion at Normandy and other coastal cities, and managed the Allied Forces to victory over Hitler and the Nazi regime. For me, the city of Brussels reflected strength. My first view of the Allied headquarters building gave me a feeling of confirmation of all that had gone on there during the course of the many months of hostilities, and in the decisions and orders that affected me and the hundreds of thousands of other GIs in like ways and in different ways. Whatever the decisions and whatever their effect, the place of origin was there. Looking at Brussels and the headquarters building in that way placed me in sort of a kindred relationship with the structure and its inhabitants. A casual tour of the building solidified all of that. There was plenty there for an intelligent conversation. It was an excellent choice for a stop in a region where some of the most brutal fighting in the war occurred; and the performance of the men of the Red Ball Express factored heavily in the effort to destroy enemy forces. "Belgium, we

adored you from the beginning," I said, as we departed her capital on the second leg of our journey.

Paris was our next destination with mini-stops at a number of small French towns en route. Now, à l'égard de (with regard to) Paris, everyone was anxious to get there, but we didn't want to miss out on the demonstration of hospitality, the show of love and appreciation that would be exhibited at places along the way. At every stop the French people would cheer and offer thanks and best wishes. When these crowds gathered to cheer, I thought of the tattered little children, women, and old men who gathered around our team the previous December as we prepared to leave for battle and how they literally walked us toward the German border. I remembered how they urged us to do well and end the war. I heard their voices then and I understood their pain. But as we returned, I thought, "The expressions on the faces of the people today are quite different from those we saw on our way to Germany" and, of course, "for good reason." The war was over and a feeling of peace was all around. What made that day in our travels even more poetic is that our passage to Paris took us through the city of Reims, site of the signing of the unconditional surrender by Germany on May 7, 1945, 11 weeks prior to our arrival there. A lot of thoughts swirled through my head as we observed the people in the streets and engaged some in pleasant conversation at the train stations. They waved their hands, they chanted and cheered. Some might have danced in the streets. People demonstrating their appreciation and showing love—what a wonderful feeling that promotes. Every stop on our return to French soil brought forth once again the memory of those people in the village near our training site. I could see them in the eyes of many people of Reims. The wish of all the people of France was fulfilled. And to think that I was a part of making it happen was, at times, overwhelming. I felt blessed to be in that role. Leaving the community of Reims was like leaving a group of old friends who had assembled for a hastily arranged party in their home where time is a premium and you know the revelry will continue on a while longer. Realizing our next destination was Paris, the city that many consider to be the most fabulous city in the world, one could say, for a while, our minds were in a pleasant state of confliction. We would survive that.

Still traveling by rail, we moved a little closer to Paris and the date of our departure for home (a thought that was always front and center), activated the nostalgia in all of

us. That was certainly true for me. Even the phrase "The last time I saw Paris" came to mind. It is probably true that every GI in France in the summer of '45 felt a kindred relationship with Paris, whether they entered the city or not. Their presence in the region qualified them for that feeling. I never saw Paris as I passed through France en route to Belgium and Germany. Fortunately no major battles were fought in the city of Paris itself. As a matter of fact, Paris was spared the heavy bombing of the like that rained down on many cities such as Frankfurt, Cologne, Bastogne, Dresden, and Berlin. However, when German troops were forced out of France by Allied troops in 1944, Hitler ordered certain destruction of areas of Paris. At one point he queried his troops, "Is Paris burning yet?"

No, Paris was not burning. But Paris and Parisians were suffering like the rest of their countrymen. France was, indeed, at war, and she played a large role over the years of the war in bringing the hostilities to an end. Reflecting back on that history as best we could increase our level of nostalgia. I was excited, but composed. In reality, I think that was true for all of us.

We arrived in Paris in the afternoon, excitement high, but emotions measured. It had been just 11 months prior that Allied Forces, including the French 2nd Armored Division, entered Paris in a triumphant return since German soldiers took over the city June 1940 following their invasion of Poland in 1939, and Norway, Denmark, The Netherlands, and Belgium, in the late spring of 1940. When Hitler's troops reached the French border, he was on a roll. That was then. Now, things had changed. On our route to the place where we would stay for a few days, we could see the charm of the city that so much had been written about and so many people had spoken favorably of. Even Thomas Jefferson had a few insightful things to say about the renowned City of Lights.

On arrival at our hotel, we were greeted with open arms. People cheered and there was merry making all around, more festive than a 20-year-old youngster from a small town in Louisiana had customarily experienced. Though the 22 months I had spent on the European Continent had prepared me for some things, I could handle it! My thoughts then were, "Let the good times roll." All of us had learned a little bit of the French grammar and could speak a few sentences in the language, plus most of the French people spoke English to an appreciable extent. So, communication was not an issue for anyone. Hotel staff

were very professional and accommodating. Doors were opened and we were treated royally and with respect. Food, drink, camaraderie—good times there were had by all.

One of the more exciting parts of the short stay in Paris was the lights. As we passed nearby months before, everything was in darkness. Seeing bright lights after being in the dark for a long span of time was in itself intriguing, and seeing the sites and a community so full of laughter was indeed a desirable interlude in our long trip back to the United States. Our arrival in Paris had been like a triumph and, indeed, we were able to see the Arc de Triomphe, the Eiffel Tower, and the River Seine. One had to venture within the time allotted to see the main boulevard of Paris, Avenue des Champs-Elysées, but these were there for all to view and enjoy. While we all had a desire to engage in more expressions, we accepted the fact that it was time to say "Au revoir à bientôt" (goodbye and see you soon). Our excursion to Paris was a valuable one. It enabled us to forget about some of the rigors of military life while providing opportunities for us to view historical scenes and places many of us would not likely have seen in our lifetime. For that, we commend the Army commanders for their thoughtfulness.

This pleasure trip had reached its conclusion and I said to myself, "Il taut que nous partitions" (we must leave), and leave we did. While saying goodbye to Paris, we boarded a bus to a place where we would be processed for the next leg of our long trip home. In about three hours we arrived at a U.S. Army Camp called Top Hat, still in reasonably high spirits and eager to complete the task the Army had for us there, with little to no thought of issues related to our experiences of the past year. On our first day at Camp Top Hat, we went through the usual kind of processing that groups of soldiers are subjected to when moved from one command or region to another. We were given a new set of clothing, which we didn't mind that at all. We completed all of the minor tasks on the second day and returned to our quarters (Tent City) in mid-afternoon for a period of relaxation. The weather was sunny and hot in that part of France at the time and we rolled up the sides of our tents to allow the air to flow through. Just as we had gotten comfortable, stretched out there on our cots with no thought of danger, some dummy ran down the narrow street in our area firing a weapon: "Boom! Boom! Boom!" We quickly hit the ground, looking for cover and something to fight with. Our weapons had long been turned in, and our hands were

bare. Even those guns some of us had taken from German soldiers had been put away. We were in a strange position. However, within a few minutes we learned that someone had fired blanks in the area. "What did I think about that? Dangerous," I thought, "great way for someone to get killed." Order was soon restored and we all returned to our bunks in the tents with a word of caution. "Don't do that again!"

I don't recall the rationale for firing blanks in the area. If it was a joke, it failed because there was no laughter, and if it was used as a test of some sort, I questioned its value. To this very day, more than 70 years later, I still do. Not that I'm angry about it; it's too easy to see that someone could easily and unnecessarily have been hurt by such a prank. Camp Top Hat failed with that process. But thanks for getting us on our way to the U.S.A.

After spending a week at Top Hat we were taken to a French port where we boarded a small Navy transport ship which would take us into New York Harbor. Once out to sea, we began to hear rumors about the war in the Pacific, which was still going on. One rumor had us getting 30 days leave at home and after that we would be sent to the Pacific to fight the Japanese. I didn't think much about that idea, but if those were the orders, I would be there. As it turned out, those orders changed the next day. The U. S. had dropped the atomic bomb on the Japanese city of Hiroshima. For the next six or seven days, we sailed toward New York with a sense of calm. This was a very slow ship. It couldn't move like the *Queen Elizabeth*; it took 14 days from France to the States, arriving in New York Harbor on August 13, 1945. Did we feel good on arrival? Thank God we made it.

There were no bands or crowds at the harbor to welcome us back. I didn't feel bad about that! I didn't think any of us expected that. From the deck I could see people on the streets going to and fro, attending to their daily affairs and seemingly having no thought of harm or danger whatsoever. That was a beautiful sight to me. They looked safe and that caused significant reflection on decisions I had made in Europe. I thought about my family there in New York. "Could any of these people walking out there on the streets be a relative of mine?" I wondered. Though they probably were not, I felt good anyway, content that I was back in the U.S.A. after having made a contribution to the safety of my country and others. Yes, I felt good and pretty much content, that is, until we were off the ship with no specific orders or directions for the remainder of the day.

Eventually a military escort did pick us up and took our group of 27-30 guys and delivered us to the command center at Fort Dix, New Jersey, where we were eventually assigned living quarters and given directions to the dining hall. Before coming off the ship I was careful to note that I hadn't seen any of our White counterparts on the ship. Evidently, there were none. As a matter of fact, I don't recall seeing any White soldiers in our proximity en route to New York Harbor. That did sound familiar. Everything was just like we left it, and our arrival in New Jersey further confirmed that nothing had changed. After our first day at Fort Dix, I thought, "Now would be a good time to have a post-hostilities conversation with General Eisenhower," even though there was no indication anywhere, as far as I could see, that the military was remotely considering ideas about how it treated its Black personnel. And that was a sad thought. I felt it, my comrades felt it, and I am certain that thousands of other Black service members felt it. Nevertheless, there was very little talk among us there about these issues. We were glad to be home, so we suffered through the pain, realizing we would get to it eventually.

During our first 24 hours at Fort Dix, it seemed that the Army's planning for us was happening piecemeal and that began to cause anxiety. However, the pace did pick up toward the end of the second day. Processing orders shifted gears, again, we were given new sets of clothes and a little cash for our pockets. We took group pictures and were informed that we would be transferred to other camps closer to our home towns. From there, we would be given a 30-day leave of absence with appropriate pay. This information was very helpful, as we were able to tell our families when they could expect to see us. I was delighted with the thought of getting home within a few days to see family I had been separated from for almost two years. I contacted family members in both Louisiana and New York. Of course, I would be going to Louisiana, since that was my home and the place of my induction into the service, and family was happy and anxious to see me. I would not be able to see family in the New York area for some time. They all understood the situation and were pleased. My two sisters, aunts, uncle, my grandfather, and a dozen or more cousins knew they would see me eventually, but I had to go home first.

While the people at Fort Dix finalized our papers for travel, members of our group did a variety of small things to make ourselves more presentable to family since two

years had brought about some physical changes, perhaps in height, weight, or even complexion, depending on the age of the individual. In my case I had grown a little after leaving home at the age of 18 and returned at 20. I think I wanted to look even more grown up after having been in a war zone for many months. So, the question for me was, "What could I do to look more grown up?" We all went into the barbershop, a big place with lots of barbers, the day before our departure for the trip South. The city slicker barbers were waiting. They had answers to every question one could imagine. They greeted us with courtesy, seemingly, with recognition of our status as veterans returning from war. The conversation easily moved to our purpose for being in the shop. Barbers discussed a variety of haircuts, including new styles, etc. Some in our group got the traditional, but others took the new style and a few got the process. I followed that group. When the barbers' work was done, we realized more fully how proficient they were as businessmen. They had offered a great variety of choices, but there was little mention of the significant differences in price. The process was at the higher end and I realized later I could not afford that hairstyle. At the time I guess I was cool, but I have never had my hair done that way since. Using the phrase

I picked up on Flatbush Avenue, "Enough already," I said. Nevertheless, I was ready for home.

Coming out of the barbershop I did feel ready for home. However, there was still another stop at camp we were invited to make: the PX. At the time I didn't recall ever having been in a military post exchange before, but I followed the group and it was a good experience. We were able to purchase a number of items to take home as gifts for family. The store was fully stocked with lots of wonderful items, and most of them seemed valuable with sale clerks who were very eager to sell their products. One little problem did exist, however. These returning GIs had big eyes but small pockets. Nobody seemed to have taken that into account, yet, these young guys, having been away from home for a while, tried to do the right thing. Some probably made a few mistakes while in the PX, but if so, they were honest mistakes. We had not devoted much time to financing and the study of budgeting while away. Since arriving at Fort Dix, we were becoming reoriented to civilian affairs, forgetting to some extent, the European experience. None of us were holding court on issues related to the war that just ended. And for a while, we were not thinking much about our status in the military beyond a 30-day leave. I suspect

for a little while, our subconscious may have wrestled with conscious for control of these issues.

Regardless, ultimately, this status situation, when carefully considered, would have substantial impact on the mind, body and the soul of each of us. The question for me at the time was, "What were the Army commanders thinking when they began to return Negro combat veterans and others home from Europe with a whole new experience in their portfolio? Had anyone given serious thought about the implication or even the provocation implicit in General Dwight Eisenhower's invitation to Negro soldiers in those segregated units in December of 1944? Had anyone in positions of authority thought that these Black, previously segregated, soldiers might have some expectations of their own?"

There were serious issues that had to be addressed and resolved, sooner or later. Preferably sooner. However, the reality was, this one group of Negro soldiers would, on any given day, board a train headed South where it would pass through a number of states, including Mississippi, where we were met by the appropriate Military attaché and taken to Camp Shelby for further processing. Needless to say, we were getting a bit tired by this time, but I still had hope. I will admit though, that, when our train arrived at the station in Meridian, I felt a little anguish. You see, having lived in the neighboring state of Louisiana for 18 years prior to my induction into the Army, I was well aware of the reprehensible treatment of Black people by Whites in Mississippi and the historic negative and racist behavior of Senator Theodore Bilbo. And this was years before the Civil Rights movement of the 1960s. A lot of thoughts swirled through my head on our arrival in Mississippi and remained for the time we were there. Yes! I was in the U.S. military uniform, but bad things had happened to Blacks in uniform. I was determined that it wouldn't happen to me.

Our arrival in Mississippi was uneventful. The paperwork time was relatively short and after spending one night at Shelby I was on a bus with authorized leave, some cash in my pocket, and a ticket to my home town of Minden, Louisiana. I was feeling much better then. Glad to be on that bus leaving Mississippi, but I had a back seat. Each one in our group went their separate ways, to their respective home state and town. The distance from Meridian to Minden, Louisiana was approximately 2,5 miles and the bus stopped regularly at cities and small towns. It was not the most comfortable ride, as I sat at the back of

the segregated bus, not on the back seat, but still the back of the bus. That ride would take nearly eight hours and I don't recall changing buses; drivers yes, but the bus went the distance.

That eight-hour ride provided lots of time for meditation. I managed to catch a little sleep, also. As I awakened, the bus was pulling into the space at the Minden Bus Station. The time was a few minutes past midnight. When the driver called out—Miden, I knew I was home and I knew I was blessed to be there. When I stepped off the bus a few minutes past midnight, I stepped off with a feeling that I had never experienced before. No description that I might attempt here would be adequate. It was unbelievably quiet and everything seemed safe. What a feeling! The bus driver got my duffel bag down and placed it on the ground near me. I picked it up and said thank you and turned toward a parked taxi cab whose driver walked over to assist. I was the only person getting off at the Minden stop, so the cab was for me. I gave the driver directions to my parents' home and in a very short time we were there. I took my bag, stepped up on the porch, knocked gently on the front door, and within seconds both my parents were at the door. What a wonderful moment that was. No tears and not a lot of talk.

Just basic expressions of joy. My little sister was sound asleep and we didn't wake her up. By the time I put my bag in the house, it was about one a.m. I felt bad having to wake my family at such a late hour, but they didn't mind because I was home safe. They were happy and so was I. We had a brief conversation, and then everybody went to sleep. My dad had to rise early to go to work at Hicks Wholesale Company. We would renew our conversation when he returned home from work. Conversation with my mother would begin as soon as I was awake.

I was pleasantly awakened about seven or eight in the morning by the beautiful aroma of home-cooked food. The smell of homemade biscuits, Louisiana cured smoked sausage, and home brewed coffee was more than enough to get me out of bed on my first day of return to my place of birth since leaving almost two years earlier to fight in a cause in which many Americans died. Some of them were my friends. We shared a common dream.

By the time I was up and dressed, my mother had breakfast on the table. That was a precious moment, sitting down to breakfast with my mother and little sister, Tommie Sean. Dad was already at work by this time. We would see him again later in the afternoon. The meal was just like the

times before I left for the Army and as I envisioned it would be on my return—outstanding! Nothing can compare to Louisiana homemade hot biscuits with real butter melting as you place it inside that biscuit. I had several of those while we sat around the table, looking at one another and enjoying the morning. And, of course, there was conversation. Not the overwhelming kind, but enough to be informed and informative. We were comfortable with the pace of the conversation and I was surprised to learn that my younger brother, Herman, had been drafted immediately after high school graduation and inducted into the Army.

With Herman's induction, that put all three brothers in the army. Our older brother, Jessie, was the first into the service. I learned later that Jessie served in the same area as I. Our paths might have crossed out there. In later conversations I learned that our brother-in-law, Bishop Smith, was in Italy with the 92nd division. It seems our family was pretty well represented in the service for our country, and if we were to look at the larger family, that is, the sons of my aunts and uncles who served our country during World War II, I suspect the numbers would swell significantly. You see I had lots of relatives who had boys in my age bracket when I was growing up. There was one cousin in particular that I inquired about, Clem Moore, Jr. Clem couldn't wait to be drafted and volunteered several months before I was inducted. He was in the South Pacific before I began basic training. I learned quite a bit just sitting around the breakfast table or dinner table. I appreciated that. The practice of having family meals together meant so much to me, as it was helpful in my growth and development—Mom and Dad did the right things.

While sitting there at the table having the first meal with family since my return, I learned about the status of all our family members—who was sick, who had given birth, and who had passed away. I learned about the neighbors and how they were doing. I was advised by my mother to schedule visiting time to see family and neighbors, usually starting with the older ones and the sick, gradually working to see everyone, and understand that they all would expect to see me. I just begin each day by visiting someone on that list and eventually I visited all of them.

In the afternoon Dad came home from his day's work. I was glad to see him walking up to the house. He was a big, strong, handsome, Christian man who lived by the principles of mutual respect. He was the no-nonsense kind. Fun was fine, in its place, but business was business. He

was a good provider and he protected his family. Although living in the South at the time of intense racial prejudice, he protected his family from any misuse by anyone, White or Black. I loved my dad and I am proud of who he was: a man of integrity and strength. I'm sorry that I never told him that, but I suspect he knew it. After all, I am his son.

Now that Dad was home, I could dig down further in my duffel bag to check out the few things I purchased at the PX at Fort Dix. Whatever I had for my mother and little sister had likely been distributed. At the PX, the sales people put a lot of emphasis on selling goods that were hard to get during the war, such as cigarettes, cigars, and other Tabasco goods. In cigarettes, I bought the maximum amount allowed, plus some cigars, chewing gum, candy, etc. As Dad was the only one in the house who smoked, I gave him all the Tabasco goods. Although he only smoked cigars, he shared the cigarettes with his friends. The other item I was most proud to give my dad was a 32-caliber pistol that I brought home from Europe, a German-made automatic, easy-to-handle weapon that would most likely be carried by a German officer as a second firearm. The German 9 millimeter Luger, an automatic pistol, was the most popular weapon associated with German officers. Everybody was on the hunt for one of them. Dad was pleased with the gift I brought home. He might have been a little surprised about the weapon, although firearms were not something new to our household.

As the gifts were distributed, I talked a little bit about my travels. He didn't ask the heavy questions: When questions were asked, I tried to provide factual and most appropriate responses. I spoke voluntarily about the people and their culture, while identifying the various countries I served in. We never talked in depth about any aspect of combat. They knew I had been in combat, but I don't remember telling them the specifics of how that came about. I am sorry that I did not explain that. I'm comfortable now sharing it all with my family, my countrymen, and others. Although family, weren't really gabby as we talked, but communication between us was consistently good. Dad reiterated the need to visit the relatives, especially those who were ill or couldn't get about on their own. My response to his suggestions were as always, "Yessir!"

As Dad and I concluded our basic conversation for the evening, I realized I had a lot of contacts to make, a lot of news to catch up on. I had a 30-day furlough, which was ample time to do the things I needed to do. I started by

visiting my aunts and my uncles and the older relatives first, then I made courtesy visits at the homes of friends and long-time neighbors. The system worked well. Then my dad made transportation arrangements for me to visit the young lady I called my girlfriend. She and her family lived several miles away, near the edge of our little town, and transportation was super. I had a very pleasant visit with Lois and her little brothers and sisters. Every contact and every conversation I had with family and friends made me feel good and helped me to have a more enriching perspective about my role in helping to bring the war to end.

My 30-day furlough ended and I returned to Camp Shelby as ordered. Within hours of my return I received orders which included an additional leave of 15 days, effective the following day. This order required that I report to Camp Polk, Louisiana, on completion of the 15 days. While I was happy for the opportunity to spend more time home with family and friends, I began to think more about our status in the army and about certain issues our group had been subjected to along the way that were not consistent with elements of fair play. I began to think about experiences in Europe and the ultimate sacrifice that some in our group had-made, and that made me sad. But, to be sure, I made every effort to conceal those feelings from family and friends. I didn't want to do anything to cause sadness or pain for them. I think I handled that very well. However, the army didn't do anything to help my situation in that regard. For, during the course of my travel from camp to home, home to camp, and back again, I was never given any information about what was happening with regard to my military status. Nobody seemed to give a damn. And yes, I understood "this is the army," as the saying goes, but what is a 20-year old lad, just returning from 22 months duty in a foreign country to think or do? In my case, I didn't do much. But I did exercise my freedom to think. Aware that the war was over in both the European and Pacific Theaters, I assumed that at some time in the relatively near future I would be honorably discharged from the service in concert with others who had served their country at home and abroad. Perhaps there would be a ceremony that attracted local community, etc. But no one had come to me or given me a piece of paper that informed me of my status and what I should expect to occur at any time in the near or distant future.

Ambrose Brodus, Jr. with rifle, in Luxemburg

Chapter 6

*Pvt. Ambrose Brodus, Jr., a few days after his return home
from WWII in Europe*

Group photo of 27 combat Infantry men at Fort Dix,
New Jersey the day following their return from Europe,
August 15, 1945

I spent the additional 15 days at home in Minden
with my family and reported to Camp Polk, Louisiana as
ordered, where I met up with my buddies from the 14th
Armored Division (the Negro Infantry Volunteers). I was
surprised, yet happy to see them. They didn't seem to know
any more than I did about our situation. We were getting
a bit edgy. It was mid-October now and the temperature
in southern Louisiana at the time was very hot. And there
we were, wrapped tightly in a totally segregated situation,

having no information about anything of value and unable to get the attention of anyone in a position of authority. The feeling of being left out was coming on fast.

14 Armored Division Insignia
Ambrose Brodus Jr. was assigned to the 14th Armored Division as an Infantryman when he volunteered for combat duty December 25, 1944

A Dastardly Act

CHAPTER 7

AN HONORABLE DISCHARGE IN A DISHONORABLE MANNER

I soon noticed that our Camp Polk quarters began to fill with other Negro soldiers. The latest group to arrive was with a quartermaster-trucking unit. In retrospect, that fact was a clue to our fate. I kept observing, and the more I observed the more assured I became that my buddies and I would not be allowed to continue in a military service configuration such as that implicit in General Eisenhower's invitation to us at the time of the Battle of the Bulge. A close examination of American history will reveal that the template for action about to be taken in the case of this group of Negro combat veterans at Camp Polk in November 1945 was, in fact, designed by the newly commissioned Commander in Chief General George Washington, at the conclusion of successful battles against the British during the Colonial War.

Finally, we were informed that we were being processed for discharge. The following day, my friends and I from the 14th Armored Division, 19th Armored Infantry Battalion, received the document which identified us as members of the 395th Quartermaster Trucking Company, Army of the United States, and stated that we were "Hereby Honorably Discharged from the Military Service of the United States of America." This discharge was shocking. I was amazed, with anguish, that we were treated in this manner. Combat, armored infantry veterans, assigned to a service company at the end of their military careers and never provided the opportunity to discuss issues or be informed of the army's plans for us. And no mention was made of anyone's intent to begin planning for the integration of the army to eliminate segregation and second-class citizenship in the Armed Services. What a blast. What were the generals thinking? Did they think we had no expectations? What happened to us was *surreptitious, dastardly, and unforgiving!*

It was consistent with the performance of George Washington in the late 1780s following the call to arms during the Revolutionary War where many runaway slaves and free Blacks took up arms to fight in the revolutionary cause. Promises were made to those Blacks who fought on

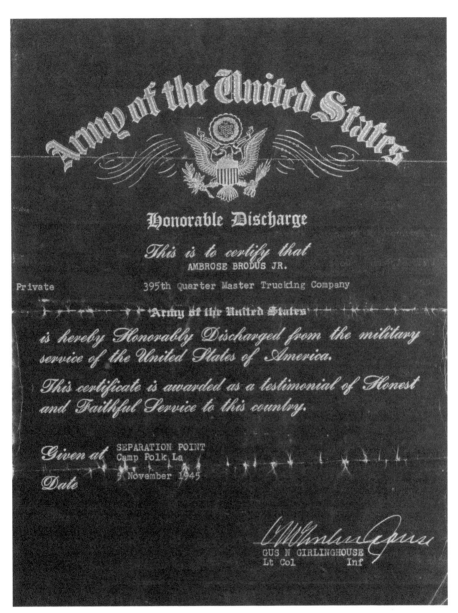

Discharge presented to Ambrose Brodus Jr., November 5, 1945 at Camp Polk, La. A DASTARDLY ACT indeed.

the side of the Colonies. However, the records show that George Washington, the Commander in Chief, issued an order at the end of the war that effectively stopped any effort to "promote, enlist or upgrade the status of Blacks in the Continental Army" at any future time. Benjamin Banneker, a free Black citizen of Baltimore and proficient scientist, spoke up in support of the free Blacks and runaway slaves who had fought in Washington's army, but his voice produced no positive results. Nobody else seemed to care about feelings and expectations, nor the promises made to the free Blacks and slaves who put their lives at greater risk to help the cause of freedom! Those in positions of authority didn't give a damn then, and more than 160 years later, the same attitude prevailed. That race was the factor in both instances is clearly evident.

While some ignorant persons, unaware of the facts and void of interest in acquiring knowledge, might attempt to argue that Blacks had paid no dues in battle or had never demonstrated fighting skills in war; their premise, in all instances, is full of holes and unworthy of a discussion at any level. However, a brief introduction to a few Blacks from earlier times and going forward might generate some interest among them and justify the time spent on such an issue.

Slavery existed during the period when colonial leaders decided to take action against the British who had imposed what the Colonies felt was unfair taxation, or "taxation without representation." The British persevered. The Colonies armed and hostilities expanded. The very first American to die in battle in the dispute with the British was a runaway slave and sailor by the name of Crispus Attucks. On March 5, 1770, following the long dispute between British soldiers and Boston citizens, Attucks came upon a scene where British soldiers had attacked a local citizen. Attucks led a charge against the soldiers and was killed. Before his death, he had yelled, "Get rid of the hated British."

Heeding the call to arms in direct response to Paul Revere, former slaves Pomp Blackman and Prince Estabrook, immediately became involved in the action. Blackmon paid for his patriotism with his life.

At the Battle of Bunker Hill, one might have heard voices of Black Patriots Peter Salem, Barzillai Lew, and Salem Poor saying, "Right on, brother," as they distinguished themselves in battle.

A Dastardly Act

In addition, the Civil War era provided ample opportunity for Blacks to gain experience in combat and demonstrate skills required of a successful soldier, and most definitely for a worthy cause, although there were, in many circles, concern and strong objections to training and arming Blacks, then giving them full authority to fight. Nevertheless, Blacks did gain those privileges and during the course of the war went on to distinguish themselves in major battles. The 54th Massachusetts Volunteer Infantry Regiment was a leader among these units. Some scholars, analyzing the contributions of Blacks in the war against the Confederacy, list the number who served at approximately 179,000. Scholars like Joseph T. Glattaar construed that the timely and extensive support of African American soldiers in the Union Army's effort tipped the scales in favor of the Union.

In 1862, President Abraham Lincoln acknowledged the value of liberating slaves in Confederate states and enlisting Blacks into service in the Northern states. There were numerous small but very significant battles in Confederate territory that were won by Black soldiers who were determined to show that they could fight as well as anybody. Black soldiers had success in major battles as well. Records show that Black soldiers fought in every military theatre: the East, West, Mississippi Valley, and the Trans-Mississippi, entering combat as early as October 29, 1862, and continuing until May 12, 1865. The 1st and 2nd South Carolina Regiments were among the first to see action in the Civil War, where they, too, distinguished themselves.

The Black man's struggle for freedom, justice, and equal opportunity in America has taken many turns over the years. I accepted General Eisenhower's letter to Black troops as another avenue toward that freedom, justice, and equality that my people have sought since the day the first slave was taken ashore from the first slave ship to arrival in American waters. Participating effectively in combat should have helped to propel that process of acquiring the status we sought. My thoughts there were no different from those of the many other Black men who went to battle for country. Black men fought and died in every war in which America has engaged in.

In World War I, Black soldiers eventually got the chance to engage in combat with the enemy due largely to unrelenting efforts of strong Black civilian organizations and powerful liberal White groups. The 369th, 370th, 371st, and the 372nd Regiments were among the first Black

Troops to see action in France. The 369th was the first army of Allied units to reach the Rhine River in Germany. Several Black infantry units were attached to the 10th Division of the French Army and distinguished themselves in battle. The 367th, known as the Harlem Hellfighters, were awarded the French Croix de Guerre for gallantry. The 92nd and the famous 93rd Division Buffalo Regiment saw combat in the St. Dil sector and the Argonne. General John J. Pershing, Commander in Chief of the American Expeditionary Force, had high praise for troops of the 92nd Division.

Black soldiers in France during WWI fought the enemy there with the full knowledge that "Jim Crow" was alive and well at home in America. Yet they persevered. In any conflict, we have demanded some of the action. We fight, we kill, we die. And still we are asked to prove ourselves. I look at history and grow weary. What's the game?

On that warm day at Camp Polk in 1945, we took our Honorable Discharge with consternation. I looked at this situation with pity. Not with pity for myself, even though I felt bad because of the insensitivity of my country toward us and the many others like us who had become victims like many others before. I knew "change" would come. Change would come because of faith, determination, and our willingness to pursue it. And there would be those strong, thoughtful voices out there in those Black organizations like the NAACP (National Association for the Advancement of Colored People). There would be those Black writers and Black editors from the Black owned newspapers and other publications in cities like Chicago, Philadelphia, Pittsburgh, and Los Angeles. I knew the powerful voices of Black men like A. Philip Randolph, Walter White, and Roy Wilkins, and U.S. Congressmen William Dawson and Adam Clayton Powell, Jr. would be heard. And the general demand for fair treatment expressed by Black soldiers returning home from service around the world would be a significant factor.

Infantryman Badge
Ambrose Brodus Jr. received this badge at the time of his
discharge from the Army, November 5, 1945

A Dastardly Act

Ambrose Brodus Jr. received this bronze star by mail from the Department of the Army, August 29, 1994, forty-nine years after his discharge from the Army at Camp Polk, LA.

CHAPTER 8

ON WITH LIFE AND HOPE FOR A BETTER FUTURE

So when we boarded trains and buses that day, going our separate ways, moving silently, never to forget the day; we parted with the understanding that "what is desired is also possible." I returned home to my family and, after taking some refresher courses to get back on track academically, I enrolled in college. Upon graduation spent 13 years in industry while also devoting quality time to issues related to civil rights. I eventually became a full time community activist as a staff member of the San Diego Urban League.

When I enrolled in Lincoln University in Jefferson City, Missouri, Black veterans were filling college campuses all over the nation and many were attending segregated schools such as Lincoln. It was a pleasant sight to see so many students with military experience on campuses from Georgia to California. Everyone knew what had to be done.

Everyone went about his own business, taking care of it. In the meantime, so much negative stuff had happened in cities across the country, many Whites resented the efforts of Blacks to improve their own status in life. Riots and lynchings cheated America out of what could have been a more joyful time for all at the end of a major war, but that was not going to happen, as racial disturbances kept happening. Even so, those powerful Black voices kept talking. They continued talking with President Harry S. Truman, the man who succeeded Franklin Roosevelt following his death, at a time when I and my buddies were still heavily engaged in battles with the enemy in Germany. In retrospect, we were there in an integrated setting, the first of its kind, as U.S. Servicemen. Our Black leaders, aware of our conditions on our return home in 1945, and our subsequent discharge from military service, and seeing no change in the Army's attitude toward segregation, pressured the president. President Truman issued Executive Order 9808 in 1946 that created the President's Committee on Civil Rights. The committee was to study existing "Federal protection of civil rights and ways to improve them." In October 1947, the Committee against Jim Crow in the Military Service and

President Harry S. Truman

Training was formed by A. Phillip Randolph and Rev. Grant Reynolds.

Shortly after that, Randolph and the Rev. Reynolds got a promise from the Democratic National Committee that a statement against the segregated draft would be issued. No such action was taken. It sounded as if games were being played here, but the master of brinkmanship would have none of it! On March 22, 1948, Randolph and his group of concerned citizens met with President Truman to request his support for anti-segregation amendments to the proposed draft bill and apparently the president sat on it, as nothing happened. Time to take it a little higher.

In June 1948, Randolph formed a group called the League for Non-violent Civil Disobedience against Military Segregation. They threatened to urge Blacks to resist induction into the military by Civil disobedience unless segregation and discrimination in the Armed Forces were banned. President Truman, being the savvy old guy some people gave him credit to be, acknowledged Randolph's political strength, and in July issued Executive Order 9981, barring segregation in the Armed Forces and created the President's Committee on Equality and Treatment of Opportunity in the Armed Services. Blacks serving on that committee with Randolph were Lester Granger, Executive Secretary, National Urban League, and John Sengstacke, Editor of the *Chicago Defender*.

Now hear this: America's entry into the Korean War came less than two years following Truman's order barring segregation in the Armed Services. There was an immediate need for troops in Korea and America's troop resource pool was in good shape as the draft was still functioning. If something here sounds familiar, the reader's power of discernment is more than satisfactory. The struggle for equality of opportunity and treatment in the military continued at a higher level with the president's most recent committee getting deeper into its work. During this period, I was attending classes every day trying to keep up with the professors' instructions, but I did make an effort to check out the political action in Washington, especially as it related to the Armed Services. I also made contact occasionally with the German family in Haag that I met with a few times. As I recall, they were still very enthusiastic about their American friend. I had planned to explore some concepts about certain conditions I observed among the German civilian population, but as my class work increased and my focus on class activity became more intense, I had

to dismiss any thoughts about exploring concepts of issues observed abroad. So I put that aside and never returned to it. I did regret doing that, but I had to set priorities.

As President Truman's Committee on Equality of Treatment and Opportunity in the Armed Services began its study, they found all of the horrible conditions Black troops had endured for years and yet maintained their love for this country—and time after time they stood up to face death in her defense. The committee had a task and they got on it and got it right. They issued a report in May 1950, titled "Freedom to Serve," which called for equality of opportunity in the Armed Services. It seems that the demands of the Korean War, which was heating up about this time, moved implementation of "Freedom to Serve" into a state of reality. People in positions of authority and responsibility started acting responsibly. And significant things related to the issue of equality and opportunity started getting done. Thanks to the president for eventually exercising his authority to do the right thing.

Without question, there were a lot of dedicated power brokers in the civilian population who put forth their best effort, during these times and earlier, to promote change in the Armed Services. And in my view, A. Philip Randolph stands at the top of the very impressive list of determined Americans who refused to accept "No" or Not yet" for answers. By 1950, many veterans from the wars in Europe and the Pacific who had entered college on the return home were beginning to graduate by large numbers. As hostilities increased in Korea, so did the demands for combat-ready troops. It seemed unlikely that many of those guys would elect to drop out of school at this time in their preparation for a career and return to a war zone. The fact is, some did. I have no numbers or percentages to provide, but one close friend of mine who had served in the Pacific zone before WWII ended, left Lincoln University in the spring of 1950 to re-enter the service. The next we heard he was in Korea.

It became evident that conditions in the military were improving. Newspaper accounts of development and over-the-fence conversations with neighbors, plus TV news, often reflected such. With regard to identifying specific areas of the military for change, one observer from a distance suggested dumping the whole plan and starting over. Of course that wouldn't happen, but there were some critical areas in the minds of many that required immediate attention. Some of those included: officer training (all phases), military police (training and utilization), fair treatment in military courts,

troop integration, and access to facilities. It was essential that all officers understand the terms "Freedom to Serve" and "Equality of Opportunity." Based on my observations, most White officers would require fundamental training with regard to fair treatment. Fortunately, there were military people, Black and White, who wanted this to work. Some lessons had been learned already and much more was to come. The time of the White master with the raised right arm saying "Stop, no 'colored' allowed!" was becoming history. To be sure, there were bumps in the road and bruises for many. But remember this: the president had spoken, an order was in place, a plan determined, and a dedicated portion of the nation's population vigorously supported the move. And lest one forget, along the way, many men died for this right to change. Of course, getting to this point required the re-education of a lot of people; that was integral.

Much has happened in the world since December of 1944 when the Fuhrer's hand-picked military experts and most notorious men of war—including General Alfred Jodl, Field Marshall Gerd von Ronsled, Field Marshall Walter Model, General Josef "Sepp" Dietrich (6th S.S. Panzer Army), and General Hasso von Manteuffel—surreptitiously launched that thunderous counter-offensive against Allied

Chapter 8

Forces in the bitter cold winter in the Ardennes of Belgium when American infantry units were decimated. Thousands of soldiers were killed in blitzkrieg-style warfare that set in motion a broad range of actions whose reverberating effects still impact the lives of people today in various ways.

Many things have changed since then because somebody made the right calls. Furthermore, President Truman's executive order began the creation of a military force that is second to none and is now integrated, with fair treatment and equal opportunity for all. It can never be said too often that "somebody paid a price for that."

When I arrived at Camp Beauregard in June of 1943 to begin a journey to acquire the skills that would enable me to make a meaningful contribution to my country's war effort, I didn't have an opportunity to select the branch of service, category of training, or type of unit I would like to be part of. In fact, nobody asked my opinion on anything. Instead, I was assigned to a group that would be trained for engineering tasks. There was little or no chance for me to request changing to something else, such as maybe, infantry—the guys who, in times of battle, are often positioned between the enemy and everybody else. I took what the Army gave me and, like the free Blacks of 1776,

made the best effort to be effective with that while searching for other opportunities.

Years passed and I still wasn't talking much about my European experience. While I observed many of my associates and some close friends becoming actively involved in veterans organizations such as the Veterans of Foreign Wars (VFW) and the American Legion, I remained on the sideline as far as participation. For a long time, it was difficult for me to consider even attending a social event organized by veterans' groups. The experience of November 1945 was still fresh in my mind. I acknowledged all of the wonderful work that A. Phillip Randolph's group and others had done, and I applauded the accomplishments being made in the Armed Forces, especially the Army. Clearly, there was very significant progress, but for the longest time, nowhere in our government was there any indication that anybody gave a damn about those Black soldiers who fought the enemy in Europe and returned to our country to face insults and deprivation. Nowhere had there been any act of reconciliation. That is, until the guy from Arkansas was elected President. When William Jefferson Clinton became 42nd President of the United States in 1993, some things changed. That is undeniable.

CHAPTER 9

AT LAST: RECOGNITION AND APPRECIATION

W hile there were some veterans of the European experience who, like me, no doubt, went about their business during the early post-WWII period, giving an occasional thought to the injustice we experienced on our return to the United States at the end of the war, there was one among the volunteers who, in time, decided to organize. His name: J. Cameron Wade, founder and chairman of the Association of the 2,221 Negro Infantry Volunteers of World War II. Wade's commitment to gain recognition for the Black soldiers from those segregated units who volunteered to face death for country is deserving of high recognition in itself. His efforts got the attention of President Bill Clinton, who first acknowledged the role of Black veterans in WWII in his appearance before the 24th Annual Congressional Black Caucus in 1995. And in 1997, the Pentagon Hall of

Heroes where Wade and other men of the Association were honored in a ceremony that paid tribute to service members whose gallantry had been overlooked for too long.

These efforts to correct a wrong inflicted on Black service members began to move at a faster pace now. The U.S. Army commissioned Shaw University to conduct a study about why no Blacks had been recommended to receive the Medal of Honor. The study determined that the racial climate and practices within the army were prohibiting factors. Numerous instances of heroic actions by African American soldiers in combat that were never officially reported were identified. As a result of these studies, seven Medals of Honor were awarded.

In the ceremony honoring the seven African American soldiers, four of whom were killed in action and two of whom died before the 1997 ceremony, President Clinton said, "Today we fill the gap in that picture and give a group of heroes, who also love peace but adapted themselves to war, the tribute that has always been their due." The President continued: "Now and forever, the truth will be known about these African Americans who gave so much that the rest of us might be free." Vernon Baker at 77 was the sole living recipient.

Chapter 9

After half-century, recognition

When their country called during WWII, blacks responded. Then Uncle Sam turned his back.

by Steven Komarow
USA TODAY

WASHINGTON - In December 1944, Nazi Germany launched its last major counteroffensive of World War II. The surprise attack into Belgium knocked Allied forces back along a 50-mile front that became known as The Bulge.

The snowy hills of the Ardennes Forests were painted with American blood. Several U.S. divisions were devastated and could not continue without an infusion of men. Time was short. So Gen. Dwight Eisenhower took an unprecedented step: He suspended racial segregation so that black troops already in Europe could replenish the all-white infantry.

"Every available weapon at our disposal must be brought upon the enemy," said an order to the "Commanders of Colored Troops" that was dated Dec. 26, 1944.

Within days, the Army had more than 4,500 volunteers from all-black units that had been relegated to support roles, such as supply.

In many cases, volunteering meant a rank reduction: blacks could serve with whites only at the lowest ranks of private and private first class.

More than five decades later, a Pentagon ceremony Thursday will honor five of those volunteers, giving them a chance to tell how proudly they fought, only to face rejection when no longer needed.

Of 2,500 black volunteers accepted for refresher weapons training in 1944, 2,221 passed. Soon they were fighting shoulder to shoulder across Europe with white troops who welcomed the help.

Upon joining its unit east of the Rhine River in March, 1945, Vincent Malveaux's platoon "was greeted by a white lieutenant who offered the colored volunteers a share in all the privileges and the hardships which service in his company might afford," says a summary

of Malveaux's testimony before an Army panel studying the integration of black and white infantry in October 1945.

In battle, race was almost never an issue. "Chow was served in mess kits, and no water was available to wash them. However, they passed from one man to another without distinction as to race."

Malveaux's platoon commander and his platoon sergeant were Southerners, "but no racial issues were raised," the summary says.

"During the first day's action the witness's platoon lost 10 men from all causes, two of whom were killed by a German mortar barrage."

Malveaux and other black infantrymen continued fighting proudly until Germany surrendered in May 1945.

But within months, most were leaving the Army in disgust. The occupation of Germany brought mistreatment by white troops who hadn't shared the battlefield with them.

And the Army bureaucracy moved quickly to resegregate the ranks.

"When they enticed us to volunteer, they said that the units we were going into would be our permanent units when the war was over," recalls J. Cameron Wade, 73, a retired Internal Revenue Service employee who lives in Irving, Texas.

"A lot of other things they said" turned out to be untrue, Wade said.

Despite glowing reviews of their effectiveness, despite the fact that they died or were wounded by the hundreds in the final push to crush Adolf Hitler's troops, the black soldiers were taken out of the infantry and put back into all-black service units.

As a further insult, the Army refused to restore the rank of those who had been demoted.

Brigadier Gen. Benjamin O. Davis, then the Army's only black general, recommended in August 1945, that the men be returned to the infantry.

"The colored soldier does not feel that he fought for a continuance of discrimination and segregation," Davis wrote after visiting black troops in Le Havre, France, who were threatening a sit-down strike because they weren't assigned to combat units.

But it wasn't until three years later that President Truman issued his historic order desegregating the military.

By then, most of the 2,221 volunteers had left the Army for good.

Many found that their discharge papers made no mention of their combat duty. And for years their unique contribution to the war remained nearly unknown to most people.

In recent years, the 2,221 volunteers, and other contributions by blacks during World War II, have been getting more public attention.

Thursday, in the Pentagon's Hall of Heroes, Gen. William Crouch, the Army's deputy chief of staff, will hold a ceremony honoring Wade, Malveaux -- who lives in the Bronx, N.Y. -- and three other members of the 2,221.

Exactly why they never received the medals is unclear. A decision to give the Bronze Star to all World War II combat infantrymen and medics was made in 1949, well after the war.

But many soldiers -- black and white -- probably never heard about it. Some of the volunteers may have applied and received them earlier.

Wade, who was awarded the Purple Heart during the war for injuries he suffered in a mortar attack, does not fault the Army today.

Four years ago, he started the Association of the 2,221 Negro Volunteers, whose four-dozen members will reunite this week in Washington.

He hopes Thursday's ceremony will spur others to apply for long-overdue honors.

Karl Schneider, the deputy assistant secretary of the Army who oversees records, says 14,000 veterans request corrections to their records in a year.

Many of them are from World War II, when the end of the fighting saw millions of men discharged within a few months.

Even though it has taken 53 years, Malveaux says getting the recognition now is important: "I was always aware that it was an injustice, and injustices can be corrected."

*Article from USA Today, July 20, 1998
regarding the substance of this book*

Mr. Clinton was at his best during that ceremony in 1997. I recall getting a glimpse of that offering on the evening news, sitting in our family room at home in San Diego, in complete amazement that this was happening. I was definitely unaware that such would be going on. Accounts of the ceremony were carried in some local newspapers the following day. Inasmuch as the activity I had observed in the nation's Capital was precisely about issues I harbored for years, I naturally clipped the article from the newspaper and stored it with the other thousands of notes that I had accumulated over the years. Obviously, I was very pleased with what I saw on television and read in the daily paper. However, I didn't discuss what I saw and read with anybody, not sure that anyone would care much. I did acknowledge later that not mentioning this historic event was not a good position for me to take.

More time passed and years later I became a little less ambivalent about things related to the U.S. Military. Then one morning in the month of July 2007, I received a phone call. The person on the line identified herself as Mae Bell-Campbell and she was trying to locate "Mr. Ambrose Brodus." When she realized that I was, in fact, the person she was looking for, she let out a big sigh of relief, seemingly

President Bill J. Clinton

happy that she had found this person. Her delight was so obvious as she explained to me her reason for calling. She represented the Association of 2,221 Negro Infantry Volunteers of WWII, who recently had organized for a certain obvious reason. When I confirmed that I was, indeed, one of the volunteers who had responded to General Eisenhower's call, her expression of joy excited me. Mae Bell explained that the group would be meeting in Nashville, Tennessee in November, around Veterans Day, and they would March in the Veterans Day parade in downtown Nashville—and I was invited. When this lady finished speaking, I was so sure that I would be in Nashville to participate with those guys as I was in December 1944, after hearing the general's call for help. I received additional information about scheduled events in Tennessee a few days later, and soon after that Lois and I were busy planning for the trip. We arrived in Nashville the day before formal events began and, from the moment we were off the plane and started toward the designated local vehicles for the ride to our hotel, we observed smiling faces of friendly people who made the same assumptions as we: that we were there for the same purpose. We all were right and, from that moment on, it was like being among long-lost, loving family.

Chapter 9

The well-dressed, elderly lady who was the first to get our attention as we hastily made our way to the ground transportation, we later discovered was the mother of the same Mae Bell who had successfully reached me that July morning with a profound message. What a message that was. And there we were, on this day, a few short months later, face-to-face with the progenitor of the woman and a clan who would make it a life's work informing a nation while promoting the cause of the 2,221. I learned a lot during the short bus ride from the airport to our hotel and the spirit of '44 flourished within me continually.

On our arrival at the hotel, I noticed a few African American gentlemen about my age bracket, moving sprightly about and I said to myself, "Comrades." The well-dressed little lady with whom we shared the bus ride from the airport helped to facilitate our check-in at the registration desk. Her name: Mrs. Annie Gill, corresponding secretary of the Association of the 2,221 Negro Infantry Volunteers. With our registration and room assignment established, the pace of activity seemed to pick up. By the time Lois and I had unpacked our bags, there was a brisk knock on the door.

If your guess is, "Mae Bell," you go to the head of the class. There she was, standing before me in person and,

like the dedicated trooper she was, informing us of the full schedule of events ahead. She did it with aplomb. Her passion for the work she was committed to was evident with each expression. We got the complete information package in a most desirable manner—from the executive director of the association. She had been elected to the position some years before, after having waged a campaign to get recognition for her uncle, Sgt. Allie S. Cottrell, who was also a 2,221 Volunteer. Mae Bell, who is now Mrs. Mae Hawkins, the wife of Anthony Hawkins of Washington, D.C., is dedicated to keeping the dream of the 2,221 Negro Infantry Volunteers alive.

The fifth reunion of the 2,221 Volunteers went off without a hitch. Three wonderful days of glorious activities and the general citizenry of Nashville and local communities, highlighted by the Veterans Day Parade was, for me, incomparable. It was the first Veterans Parade I had ever been a part of. Events were well organized and I met a lot of friends and patriotic people who seemed to understand better than some others what America is about. Above all, I had the opportunity and pleasure of meeting people who had the same idea as I when their "Colored"

Comrades of WWII from left to right:
Arthur Betts, Chicago, Illinois
Matthew Brown, Savannah, Georgia
Ambrose Brodus, Jr., San Diego, CA
Oscar Osborne, New York City

(segregated) units in December 1944 received the call from General Eisenhower.

There are a few words that can describe the feeling I had when, after all of those years, I had the opportunity to shake hands with veterans who once shared many of the same experiences and circumstances as I. It was very refreshing to be able to sit and talk for a while about some of the things we were exposed to and to take a reflective view

From Left to Right: Milton Graham, Oscar Osborne, Lawrence Brown, Ambrose Brodus, Jr.

From Left to Right: Lois Brodus, Shoshana Johnson (1st female American prisoner of the Iraq War), Ambrose Brodus, Jr.

of how some things were handled. The fact of our presence, enjoying and appreciating the camaraderie, fully aware of the past but in command of the present, was grand. At that moment I was reminded of a song that one of the groups at our church sing now and then something—something about the ups and downs and the hard times, but we made it, "Thank God! We made it!" We have a lot to be thankful for, I was thinking. My attendance at the reunion of the 2,221 Negro Infantry Volunteers and my active participation in the Veterans Day Parade inspired me to take all necessary and appropriate measures to inform my family, my community, and the nation about my experiences in WWII, as it is a phase of American History most people seem to know little about. Furthermore, the trip to Nashville in 2007 secured from me a commitment to promote the goals and objectives of the 2,221 and to take an active role in veterans' affairs, including maintaining active membership in the American Legion.

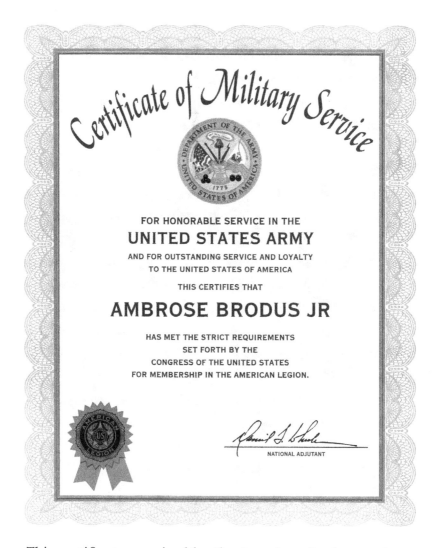

This certificate acquired by the American Legion confirms Ambrose Brodus Jr.'s commitment to become involved with Veterans programs

CHAPTER 10
REFLECTIONS OF GRADUAL PROGRESS

One spring day in 1944, while on maneuvers in the Moor in England with my engineering company, months before General Dwight D. Eisenhower made his decision on the time to "go," I observed from a distance an all-White unit in our vicinity moving sort of obliquely in a direction away from my company. I thought that was a bit unusual, seeing them in relatively close proximity to this African American group, even while passing on the highway. During the first few months I had been there, I didn't recall ever seeing Black and White troops trying to occupy the same space, except perhaps at a time when there was a goof in scheduling, and those were usually off-duty times which often resulted in racial conflict. And racial conflict did occur, perhaps more frequently in the metropolitan areas of England (wherever it happened, it was bad and ugly). Thinking as I always did about racial issues in the U.S. Armed Services, I wondered

again and again about how much more productive and efficient, and how much fairer, the services would be if the problem of segregation in the services were eliminated.

President Harry Truman's Executive Order 9981 of July 1948, barring segregation in the Armed Forces, effectively addressed that issue and, by the end of the Korean War, the military was on its way to becoming the entity that Randolph and his League for Non-violent Civil Disobedience Against Military Segregation had in mind. Without question, the Armed Forces were on their way, but not there yet. And the eyes of the brothers were upon it, even to the present day.

At the time of WWII, there was just one African American General, Benjamin O. Davis, Sr. At the end of 1954 America had its second African American General, Benjamin O. Davis, Jr. During WWII, 1,085,539 Blacks were drafted into the Armed Forces and 125,000 of them served overseas. Approximately one million served in the Army, fewer were in the Navy, 18,000 in the Marine Corps, and 5,000 served in the Coast Guard. As of 2016, there were approximately 2.6 million African American veterans. The U.S. Military is about 20% Black today. During the Korean and Vietnam Wars, some felt that Blacks were overrepresented in combat units, clearly a reflection of the effort and progress at that time.

Black Officer Firsts

- First Black General: Benjamin O. Davis, Sr. in 1940 (Army). The second Black general was his son, Benjamin O. Davis, Jr., in 1954 (Air Force), and the third was Roscoe C. Cartwright in 1971 (Army).

- First Black Army Female General: Hazel W. Johnson in 1979.

- First Black Navy Admiral: Samuel L. Gravely, Jr. in 1971.

- First Black Marine Corps General: Frank E. Petersen in 1979.

More History

- In 1973, there were 12 Black Army generals, 3 Air Force generals, and 1 Navy Admiral.

- By 1997, 7.5% of military officers were Black (6.5% in 1987).

According to Pentagon data as of May 2008:

- 5.6 percent of the 923 general officers or admirals were Black.

- Eight Blacks were three-star lieutenant generals or vice admirals.

- Seventeen were two-star major generals or rear admirals.

- Twenty-six were one-star brigadier generals or rear admirals.

- Three of the Black one-stars were women.

- There have been 11 black 4-star rank officers: one in the Navy, five in the Army, and five in the Air Force. The first was the Air Force's Daniel "Chappie" James in 1975. Currently, the only Black 4-star general is the Army's William E. "Kip" Ward, commander of U.S. Africa Command.

- Marines: It is a little known fact that there have been 16 Black Marine Corps generals. That statistic speaks volumes for the Corps, which is the smallest of the U.S. military units.

- The summer of 2014 marked the first time a female had been appointed to be a 4-star Admiral in the Navy. Michelle Howard became the first Female, and the first Black Female, to receive 4 stars.

What has happened in the United States Military since 1948 is nearly miraculous. Equal opportunity and fair treatment is just about a given today. It has come to be this way because someone now cares. However, policies, programs, conditions, and activities must be monitored and adjusted continuously to ensure that we, as citizens of this

Chapter 10

*Admiral Michelle Howard recieving her 4-star
shoulder boards*

great country, are living up to the intent and purpose of
the Constitution. Never again should an African American
service member be treated differently from any other or to be
systematically subjected to indignities based on color, race,
class, or caste. These are essentially the principles that I
stepped forward for when General Eisenhower extended the
invitation to segregated troops at a critical time during the
war. When some friends learned of my experience after so
many years, they asked if I would do it again. My response

NAVAL TRAILBLAZER IS FIRST FEMALE FOUR-STAR ADMIRAL

MARK WALKER • U-T

History was made Tuesday when trailblazer Michelle Howard — the first black woman to captain a U.S. naval vessel when she commanded the Rushmore in San Diego in 1999 — became the Navy's first female four-star admiral.

Howard was awarded her fourth star Tuesday and also became the first woman to server as vice chief of naval operations, the No. 2 position in the sea service.

Howard made little mention of her personal achievements during a ceremony at The Women in Military Service for America Memorial at Arlington, Va., instead saluting the nation's all-volunteer military.

"Volunteerism is the core of the Unite States personal character and our national identity," she said. "The willingness to step up and contribute to a noble cause in your life is a sign of true selflessness. Our sailors and Marines are this legacy — they are volunteers and with every mission they demonstrate our core values."

Navy Secretary Ray Mabus lauded Howard and noted her elevation comes as the nation observes the 50th anniversary of the Civil Rights Act. Her promotion, he said, removes a final barrier to women.

"She is a representation of how far we have come and how far she has helped to bring us," Mabus said of the 54-year-old who was born at March Air Force Base near Riverside.

"I hope that today is an example of a Navy that now reflects the highest ideals of the nation we serve, a nation where success is not borne by ethnicity or gender but by skill and ability."

Howard's naval resume is replete with firsts and major accomplishments and recognitions, including serving in the Persian Gulf War in 1991.

She took command of the Rushmore, an amphibious dock landing ship, in March 1999 at the 32nd Street Naval Station. She later commanded a Navy amphibious squadron, and headed up and two expeditionary strike groups.

The second of those expeditionary leadership roles included commanding Task Force 151 in the spring of 2009, a multi-national counter-piracy effort where she oversaw the successful plan to rescue Capt. Richard Phillips of the Maersk Alabama, who had been taken hostage by Somali pirates.

Mabus noted that Howard's role in the film "Captain Phillips" starring Tom Hanks was done solely by a voice-over.

"You need a better agent," he joked. "That should have been you."

Howard attended high school in Aurora, Colorado, and then graduated from the U.S. Naval Academy in 1982. She entered the school at age 17 in what was the third class to accept women. She later earned a master's degree in military arts and sciences.

San Diego retired Rear Adm. Ronne Froman, the first woman to serve as commander of Navy Region Southwest, serves with Howard on a board that oversees the academy.

"She is an accomplished warfare and staff officer who has worked very, very hard and proven her mettle," Froman said.

"We didn't think the Navy would make a woman a our-star admiral until someone was qualified and she is definitely is that person.

"She doesn't take herself too seriously and she's a great person to be around," Froman continued. "Her promotion is a big deal because reaching four-star admiral is the ultimate in naval service. This is a big step for the Navy and I am so proud of her."

Froman also said Howard did a great deal to help shore up problems the amphibious ship program commanding the Rushmore.

Howard now assumes the duties as the 38th vice chief of naval operations from Adm. Mark Ferguson.

Her boss, Adm. Jonathan Greenert, chief of naval operations, said he expects more great things from her. "Michelle's many trailblazing accomplishments

Article from U-T reflectin progress in U.S. Military regarding equal opportunity

City of San Diego

Proudly
Representing the
Communities of:

- Alta Vista
- Bayview Hills
- Broadway
  Heights
-Chollas View
- Emerald Hills
- Jamacha
- Knox
- Lincoln Park
- Lomita Village
- Mount Hope
- Mt. View
- North Bay
  Terraces
- North Encanto
- O'Farrell Park
- Oak Park
- Paradise Hills
- Ridgeview
- Rosemont
- Skyline Hills
- South Bay
  Terraces
- South Encanto
- Valencia Park
- Webster
- Willie
  Henderson Area

COUNCILMEMBER ANTHONY YOUNG

Special Commendation

Presented To

2221 NEGRO INFANTRY
VOLUNTEERS of WWII
8th Annual Reunion

On behalf of the citizens of District Four and the City of San Diego,
welcome to America's Finest City as you celebrate your
8th Annual Reunion.

Your continued commitment toward our great nation and her people
is truly appreciated, especially during a time of racial discrimination.
I applaud your fortitude toward building the backbone of our great
nation.

Again, I wish you a most productive and pleasant stay in San
Diego as you rekindle old friendships, share the fondest of
memories and stand again as the proud and respected
2221 Negro Infantry Volunteers of WWII.

Anthony Young
Councilmember, Fourth District

November 10, 2010

Date

*San Diego City Councilmember Anthony Young pays tribute
to members of 2221 Negro Infantry Volunteers of WWII*

In appreciation of:

2221 Negro Infantry Volunteers of WWII

The Parade Committee, sponsors, and supporters gratefully acknowledge your Participation in this year's event. The Parade is a remarkable gathering of patriots who honor the military defenders of the United States of America. Thank You for participating in preserving the tradition of honoring our nation's heritage.

The Nation expresses it gratitude to those that protected this country during the years of the Cold War. Welcome Home Cold War Warriors.

Thank You

Jack Harkins
Jack Harkins
Veterans Week chairman

John Weaver
John Weaver
Veterans Day Parade Chairman

San Diego County Veteran's Day Parade Committee
expressed thanks to WWII Volunteers

was emphatic: "Without hesitation!" However, there would have to be some dialogue at the time of commitment to ensure all parties understood my expectations and that a firm commitment to that end was established. When that was done, we would have a deal. No more "maybe, perhaps, or I'll see what we could do" stuff. Those days left with the wind. We are equal partners in this American Citizenship business.

Further, on my return home from the foreign venture, I would seek out and immediately join hands with the current

Ambrose Brodus Jr. standing before plaque to D-Day

Words on the plaque written by
General George C. Marshall

Ambrose Brodus Jr. & Oscar Osborne, WWII Museum

Oscar Osborne at WWII Memorial

Chapter 10

A. Philip Randolphs of our national community to promote and ensure a continuing high and equitable standard for our nation's Armed Forces. I would do anything necessary to effect change that is desirable. And now that we seem to have it, I know the songwriter was right when he said, with an obvious expression of joy and relief, "It was a long time coming, but I know—change is going to come."

From my perspective, and for so many reasons, military service in those segregated units was a long way to come from. But the brothers had the audacity to perform with distinction wherever they served, knowing that America, indeed, is their country too! Sometimes now, I look back at those days of degradation and so many pieces come at me, one at a time, perhaps to test my soul. Usually I find a way to handle most of it in a flash. But there are some things that bug me still whenever my thoughts turn to fortunes or misfortunes of war. One is that condition in the central part of the text of General Eisenhower's letter to the "Colored" troops that required Black non-commissioned officers who wished to volunteer for the project to give up their rank, only privates or privates first class would be accepted. One of those soldiers who gave up his sergeant stripes was Medal of Honor recipient Vernon Baker.

From the beginning, the Volunteer Project placed the larger burden of responsibility on the shoulders of the brothers. And trust me, those of us who took up the offer were tested from the start, from the very first day of processing. But what the testers failed to understand is that we experienced the basic elements of the test long before such was assembled.

So, on those occasions when I am compelled to think through some of those negative issues of the past, especially the time of our honorable/very dishonorable discharge, a dastardly act indeed, I simply take a breath, exhale, and think about the manner in which we handled it all. And I am okay with that! I'd just like more people to know about these things.

Yes, you are beautiful, America, but you still have some ways to go.

SELECTED REFERENCES FOR A BROADER VIEW OF AMERICAN MILITARY HISTORY OF BLACK TROOPS IN WAR AND RELATED DATA

Alexander, Vern Louis. *Black Opposition to Participate in American Military Engagements from the American Revolution to Vietnam.* Denton: North Texas State University, 1978.

Alt, William E. *Black Soldiers, White Wars: Black Warriors from Antiquity to the Present.* Westport, Connecticut: Praeger, 2002.

Ash, Stephen V. *Firebrand of Liberty: The Story of Two Black Regiments that Changed the Course of the Civil War.* New York: W. W. Norton and Company, 2008.

Black, Wallace B. *Slaves to Soldiers: African American Fighting Men in the Civil War.* New York: F. Watts, 1998.

Booker, Bryan D. *African Americans in the United States Army in World War II.* Jefferson, North Carolina: McFarland and Co., 2003.

Bruseino, Thomas A. *A Nation Forged in War: How World War II Taught Americans to Get Along.* Knoxville: University of Tennessee Press, 2010.

Buckley, Gail Lumet. *American Patriots: The Story of Blacks in the Military from the Revolution to Desert Storm.* New York: Random House, 2001.

Edgerton, Robert B. *Hidden Heroism: Black Soldiers in America's Wars.* Boulder, Colorado: Westview Press, 2001.

Harris, Bill. *The Hellfighters of Harlem: American Soldiers Who Fought for the Right to Fight for Their Country.* New York: Carroll & Graf Publishers, 2002.

Hart, S., R. Hart, and M. Hughes. *The German Soldier in World War II.* London: Amber Books, 2016.

Hitler, Adolph. *Mein Kampf.* Translated by Ralph Manheim. Boston, Massachusetts: Houghton Mifflin Company, 1998.

Lentz-Smith, Adriane D. *Freedom Struggles: African Americans and World War I.* Cambridge, Massachusetts: Harvard University Press, 2009.

McCullough, David. *1776*. Waterville, Maine: Thorndike Press, 2005.

Motley, Mary P., Editor. *The Invisible Solider: The Experience of the Black Soldier, World War II*. Detroit, Michigan: Wayne State University Press, 1987.

Nankivell, John H. *Buffalo Soldier Regiment: History of the Twenty-Fifth United States Infantry, 1869-1926*. Lincoln: University of Nebraska Press, 2001.

Reader's Digest. *The World at Arms: Reader's Digest Illustrated History of World War II*. New York: Readers Digest, 1989.

Rooney, Andy. *The Fortunes of War*. Columbus, Georgia: Little, Brown, 1962.

Sasser, Charles W. *Patton's Panthers: The African American 761st Tank Battalion in World War II*. New York: Pocket Books, 2004.

Schubert, Irene, and Frank N. Schubert. *On the Trail of the Buffalo Solider II: New and Revised Biographies of African Americans in the U.S. Army*. Lanham, Maryland: Scarecrow Press, 2004.

Slotkin, Richard. *Lost Battalions: The Great War and the Crisis of American Nationality*. New York: H. Holt, 2005.

Smith, John David. *Black Soldiers in Blue: African American Troops in the Civil War Era*. Chapel Hill: University of North Carolina Press, 2003.

Wagner, Margaret E. *World War II 365 Days*. New York: Harry N. Abrams, 2009.

Wilson, Joe. *The 784th Tank Battalion in World War II: History of an African American Armored Unit in Europe*. Jefferson, North Carolina: McFarland, 2007.

Wilson, Joseph T. *The Black Phalanx: African American Soldiers in the War of Independence, the War of 1812, and the Civil War*. New York: Da Copa Press, 1994.

Wynn, Neil A. *The African American Experience During World War II*. Lanham, Maryland: Rowman and Littlefield Publishers, 2010.